# THE
# FAMILY OFFICE
## Advising the Financial Elite

Russ Alan Prince   Hannah Shaw Grove

Keith M. Bloomfield   Richard J. Flynn

The Family Office: Advising the Financial Elite
By Russ Alan Prince, Hannah Shaw Grove, Keith M. Bloomfield, Richard J. Flynn

cfpn

Charter Financial Publishing Network
499 Broad Street
Shrewsbury, NJ 07702
Phone: 732-450-8866
Fax: 732-450-8877
www.pw-mag.com

ISBN: 978-0-9800679-2-7

TO JERRY—
IN MEMORY OF HIS LOVE AND COMMITMENT.
TO JERRY—
FOR MAKING EACH DAY WONDERFUL.
*Russ Alan Prince*

FOR SEEING BEAUTY AND TRANQUILITY WHEN I COULDN'T, TO AGK.
*Hannah Shaw Grove*

TO MY FAMILY FOR THEIR UNCONDITIONAL LOVE AND SUPPORT.
*Keith M. Bloomfield*

TO MY FAMILY WITH LOVE.
*Richard J. Flynn*

# TABLE OF CONTENTS

**FOREWORD** . . . . . . . . . . . . . . . . . . . . . . . . . . . . . . . . . . . . . . . . . . . . . . . vii

**ABOUT THIS BOOK** . . . . . . . . . . . . . . . . . . . . . . . . . . . . . . . . . . . . . . . . ix

**INTERLUDE** *The Bastard of the Brothel* . . . . . . . . . . . . . . . . . . . . 11

**PART I:** The Financial Elite

**CHAPTER 1:** The Top of the Financial Pyramid . . . . . . . . . . . . . . . . 17

**CHAPTER 2:** The Roads to Riches . . . . . . . . . . . . . . . . . . . . . . . . . . . . 21

**CHAPTER 3:** Money Rules . . . . . . . . . . . . . . . . . . . . . . . . . . . . . . . . . . 27

**INTERLUDE** *The Angel Investor* . . . . . . . . . . . . . . . . . . . . . . . . . . . 39

**PART II:** The Family Office Today

**CHAPTER 4:** The Appeal of the Family Office . . . . . . . . . . . . . . . . . 47

**CHAPTER 5:** Types of Family Offices . . . . . . . . . . . . . . . . . . . . . . . . . 53

**CHAPTER 6:** Motivations and Rationale . . . . . . . . . . . . . . . . . . . . . 67

**INTERLUDE** *The Five Fingers* . . . . . . . . . . . . . . . . . . . . . . . . . . . . . 75

**PART III:** The Executive Director

**CHAPTER 7:** Perspectives on the Position . . . . . . . . . . . . . . . . . . . . 83

**CHAPTER 8:** What It Takes . . . . . . . . . . . . . . . . . . . . . . . . . . . . . . . . 91

**INTERLUDE** *The Empire Builder* . . . . . . . . . . . . . . . . . . . . . . . . . 103

**PART IV:** Wealth Management

**CHAPTER 9:** Investment Management . . . . . . . . . . . . . . . . . . . . . . 111

**CHAPTER 10:** Advanced Planning Services . . . . . . . . . . . . . . . . . . 123

**CHAPTER 11:** Private Investment Banking . . . . . . . . . . . . . . . . . . 129

**INTERLUDE**  *The Gnome* . . . . . . . . . . . . . . . . . . . . . . . . . . . . . 135

**PART V:** Support Services

CHAPTER 12:  Administrative Services . . . . . . . . . . . . . . . . . . . . . . . 143

CHAPTER 13:  Lifestyle Services . . . . . . . . . . . . . . . . . . . . . . . . . . 149

**INTERLUDE**  *The Monster Hunter* . . . . . . . . . . . . . . . . . . 155

**PART VI:** Emerging Trends

CHAPTER 14:  Turnarounds & Lift-offs . . . . . . . . . . . . . . . . . . . . 163

CHAPTER 15:  Specialty Family Offices . . . . . . . . . . . . . . . . . . . . 169

CHAPTER 16:  Leadership Transitions . . . . . . . . . . . . . . . . . . . . . 177

CHAPTER 17:  The Outpost Family Office . . . . . . . . . . . . . . . . . . 189

**INTERLUDE**  *The Mistress of the Universe* . . . . . . . . . . . . . . . 195

**APPENDICES:**

APPENDIX A:  The Advisory Migration . . . . . . . . . . . . . . . . . . . . 201

APPENDIX B:  Selecting a Multi-Family Office . . . . . . . . . . . . . . . . 203

APPENDIX C:  Executive Director Compensation at
Single-Family Offices . . . . . . . . . . . . . . . . . . . . . . 205

APPENDIX D:  The Whole Client Model . . . . . . . . . . . . . . . . . . . 211

APPENDIX E:  Sampling Methodology . . . . . . . . . . . . . . . . . . . . 212

**ABOUT THE AUTHORS** . . . . . . . . . . . . . . . . . . . . . . . . . . . . . 213

# FOREWORD

I n 2004 Russ Alan Prince and Hannah Shaw Grove published what was, at the time, the most comprehensive empirical analysis of the family office universe—a book entitled *Inside the Family Office: Managing the Fortunes of the Exceptionally Wealthy.* Admittedly, the book was written for a very small audience, and, as is often the case in such small communities, the book made its way into the hands of this select group of individuals who had either a professional or personal interest in family offices. Despite the passage of time, the book continues to serve as the seminal text on family offices and is enjoying a renaissance as these organizations influence the service approach at financial services firms and evolve to become more accessible to a larger population.

Over the past six years, Russ and Hannah emerged as the world's leading authorities on family offices and have been retained by wealthy families and select advisors for their unparalleled counsel. In the course of establishing the Forbes Family Trust, we turned to them to better understand the business challenges and for help navigating the key decisions that could affect the Trust's operational effectiveness and profitability. One byproduct of our collaboration was a shared desire to update the important research that was the basis of their first book. Russ, Hannah and their new co-authors, Keith M. Bloomfield and Richard J. Flynn, conducted an extensive research initiative with family offices that was facilitated and sponsored by the Forbes Family Trust.

*The Family Office: Advising the Financial Elite* is the culmination of their research and includes a detailed discussion of their key findings and the short and long-term implications for the family office universe. I believe it is the most thorough and insightful work on this little known, yet highly desirable, entity available in the marketplace today.

Advising the world's wealthiest individuals has always called for precision, exclusivity and adaptability and the current environment is no exception. Today the business of private wealth management is at a critical juncture in its lifecycle and I believe the authors of this book and their new research will play a meaningful role in how things take shape in the years to come.

*Miguel R. Forbes*
*Vice Chairman, Forbes Family Trust*
*New York, NY*
*May 2010*

# ABOUT THIS BOOK

In the mid-2000s, more people had more wealth than ever before fueling an interest in more personalized service and the need for more accessible financial products and strategies to address business succession, tax mitigation and risk management, among other things. Simultaneously, more companies began to focus on the affluent as a key part of their business and growth plans. Those two factors, along with a few others, helped raise awareness for things like wealth management, private banking, discretionary advice, and, of course, family offices.

Any book is the work of many people. In the case of this book, *The Family Office: Advising the Financial Elite,* it is the work of many people over many years. In 2004, we published our first book on family offices and since that time both the original book and the subject matter have experienced a boost in popularity. And in the years since the release of *Inside the Family Office: Managing the Fortunes of the Exceptionally Wealthy,* we've continued to conduct quantitative and qualitative research and publish articles and reports that tracked relevant changes and developments in the field.

This book is not a sequel, but rather a way for us to keep the dialogue about family offices front and center among the very wealthy and the firms and specialists they rely on to manage their personal and financial affairs. Like our first book, this one is based on primary research conducted with family offices and high-net-worth and ultra-high-net-worth individuals. At this point, it's worth mentioning a few things about how we do research and its implications for the data in this book.

## *Caveat Emptor, Dummy*

Researching the wealthy is a complicated and often misunderstood process. Unlike much market research that is done using random samples, there is nothing random about working with the super-rich. It takes a significant amount of time and effort to find, qualify and secure the participation of the respondents to ensure the integrity of the data; in the case of this book it took several years to build a verified sample. Frequently we turn to accepted social sciences methods that are largely unknown to the general population, such as snowball sampling (where qualified respondents help us identify other qualified respondents) or intermediary-based judgment sampling (where one person acts as the proxy to the research subject) to construct our samples. Using these types of methods can mean that a sample does a better job representing a sub-segment of the population rather than the entire population, or that the margin of error is slightly larger to allow for differences between the respondents and their peer universe. Our sample sizes are often very small when compared to, say, a consumer opinion survey or a political poll, but our findings are statistically internally valid (unless noted otherwise) and directionally correct.

## The Core Materials...

In the following pages we examine the current business structures and orientations of today's family offices, the role of the Executive Director, the platform of services and the key trends that have the potential to shape the future of high-end wealth management services. We've also chosen to expand the information about the wealthy themselves to include how the financial elite differ from middle-class millionaires, the attributes and behaviors driving most significant wealth creation and the shifting attitudes about personal wealth. These details, while interesting, also play a more meaningful role in how family offices interface with the very wealthy and deliver against specific goals and objectives.

## ... and a Few, Unexpected Bonuses

To help dimensionalize some of the data and conclusions presented in this book, between each section are Interludes—profiles, if you will, of billionaires that illustrate a particular aspect of their extraordinary approach to relationships, business and money.

Whether you're starting, managing, overhauling, assessing or working with a family office, we hope you'll find that the unique combination of our empirical and experiential research is a useful complement to your own knowledge and helps enhance your understanding of the topic. Like the rest of the financial and professional services industries, family offices are in a period of transition that bears watching. *The Family Office* contains the very latest research and unparalleled insights on the issues that will affect and shape the world of the financial elite—now and in the future.

*Russ Alan Prince and Hannah Shaw Grove*
*New York, NY*
*May 2010*

# The Bastard of the Brothel

# The Bastard of the Brothel

By Russ Alan Prince and Hannah Shaw Grove

*She sits quietly and looks straight into his eyes, feeding on his fear. Yes, it sounds like a line from a pulp novel, but the truth is, she is relishing the anxiety and suffering she's causing. The psychic damage she inflicts turns her on. The meeting lasts about an hour. They conclude by signing documents. She silently walks out with her all-female entourage of seven attorneys and bodyguards. She just earned over $120 million on this small transaction—a 600% return in less than three years.*

Twenty-five years ago...Russ sits in a rundown box of an apartment with four friends in a strange land. She's there and they're talking about what to do with their lives. While most of them discuss a variety of possibilities, some of them very altruistic, she single-mindedly wants to become rich. But rich to her is not $10 million or $100 million. She wants to be world-class, Forbes 400 wealthy. She wants to be a billionaire. Preferably a billionaire a few times over. Nothing else matters... nothing AT ALL.

## The Lesson Learned in the Whorehouse

She grew up in a whorehouse. She never knew her father. Her mother died when she was about five. Not surprisingly, her childhood is the foundation of her fixation with accumulating massive wealth. She believes that money means opportunities. Money is life. Money is the only thing that really matters. Besides, money is a girl's best friend.

For a pretty smart group, they were awfully stupid, as young adults often are. Not knowing better, they took her lead and decided to get fabulously rich. They slipped into the zeitgeist and quickly picked up on the "rules of conduct" that translate into extreme success and astronomical wealth.

Today...After following these rules with a burning passion for a quarter century, she's unquestionably a billionaire in command of a little empire dominated by women from the same world she originally came from. We've been periodically privileged, and regularly frightened, to see her in "action."

Our experiences in this milieu haven't been restricted to dealing with her. Over the years, we've ethnographically studied other self-made billionaires as well as many self-made millionaires who have not yet reached B-list status. In evaluating their attitudes, behaviors and actions when it comes to wealth creation, we've identified precise, dominant, persistent patterns— rules, if you will.

This set of rules encapsulates the strategies and tactics that can poten- tially make a person a billionaire or, at least, phenomenally affluent. Most anyone can follow these rules of conduct and achieve significantly greater personal and pecuniary success. However, it's often most effective for people who have already realized a moderate level of wealth but want to "own the stars."

We're not advocating that you follow them. Even if you choose to do so, we're certainly not advocating that you commit yourself to these rules as our protagonist has. We also want to make it very clear that people have created great fortunes without following these rules. While Russ started down this path long ago, he soon stopped and has since approached personal wealth creation very differently. As with most things in life, there are tradeoffs—just ask Faust.

# PART I

# The Financial Elite

# The Top of the
# Financial Pyramid

In the title of the book and throughout it we refer to the 'financial elite.' So who is the financial elite and how much money does it take to be considered part of this group? Defining wealth can be done in a number of ways and segmentation often plays a key role in the success of a particular initiative. In the case of family offices, it takes the right type of family with the right kinds of resources to function optimally—and knowing who and what that is becomes a critical part of the game plan.

First we drew on our years of experience studying and working with the high-net-worth markets and then weighed that against the demographics of today's single- and multi-family offices. For the purposes of *The Family Office*, we define the financial elite as individuals or families with a net worth of US$20 million or more. This level of wealth is significant enough to spawn a mindset and a lifestyle that is distinct from the garden-variety millionaire; one that craves privacy and confidentiality while demanding white glove service and leading-edge thinking from the professionals turned to for guidance and support. This level of wealth also translates to an increased likelihood to work with the wealth managers and specialist advisors who can deliver the investment, tax and financial advantages they value.

To keep this in context, a family with a net worth of US$20 million is nowhere near the top of the financial pyramid; the pinnacle of wealth is measured in billions (Exhibit 1.1). By sizing the population of individuals or family units with at least US$20 million we can be assured of including everyone that works with, is interested in, or is appropriate for the family office construct.

EXHIBIT 1.1:

## The Top of the Financial Pyramid

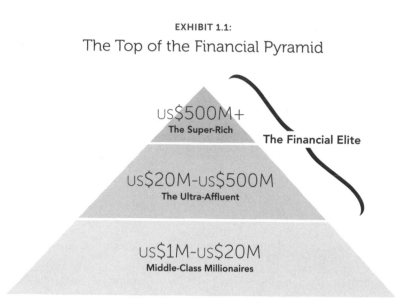

## SIZING THE POPULATION

Prince & Associates, Inc. constructed the first analytic model to estimate the size and aggregate wealth of various segments of the high-net-worth universe in 2002. We regularly update the model and the estimates to reflect the current environment, and, most recently, revised the model in light of the credit crisis, the decrease in the world's economic growth rate and related events. The current model, built in 2009, accounts for the actual and perceived differential in selected assets, such as business interests, real property and collectibles; the change in status of specific tax havens; the role of the "underground economy" on private wealth creation; and excludes wealth generated by illegal activities.

We incorporated data from 68 different sources, all of which are focused on some aspect of working with or serving the exceedingly wealthy. These sources include think tanks, financial institutions, industry consultants, academics and government organizations. Some of our sources are well known entities and others are not. The lesser-known sources are specialty providers that focus on issues unique to the super-rich, such as the management of business interests and residences in multiple countries, regulatory environments and tax jurisdictions. Some examples of these specialty providers are:

- **The Medmenham Abbey,** an advanced planning boutique that caters to the top echelon of European and US-based wealth. The Abbey has sophisticated skills and capabilities to assist their ultra-affluent clients with business interests and residences in multiple countries, regulatory environments and tax jurisdictions. The firm's roots can be traced back to the 1700's and the Friars of St. Francis of Wycombe. Many of its clientele have genealogical links to European nobility and other well-known historical figures.

- **The Soloton Society,** a comparatively larger financial and legal advisory firm as measured by the number of employees and clients, and the range of services offered. The Society has developed some particular capabilities such as allowing it to act as agent and facilitator to "professional tourists," or individuals and business people that are continually on the move and consequently have no tax obligation in many locations. The organization claims ancestral links to the Poor Knights of Christ and the Temple of Solomon.

- **Vargas Partners,** a tax-strategy firm that specializes in managing the intersection of its client's personal and business affairs. Its efforts, such as tax treaty shopping and restructuring income sources, frequently command multi-million US dollar fees. The principals of the firm trace their history back 300 years and some of the client relationships are more then a century old.

The existence of these specialty providers further reinforces the fact that the financial elite has distinct needs and operate in a different universe than the rest of the world's population—and it is this unique arena in which family offices also operate.

The analytic model allows us to calculate the number of financial elite in the world and the total wealth they control. A best estimate was calculated for each statistic along with both high and low scenarios. In the tables below we've included 2007 and 2010 figures to illustrate the change in this population in recent years. Exhibit 1.2 shows that the number of super-wealthy in the world decreased from 2007 to present day by 165,000, or 18%, though we calculated the range of decline to fall between 11%-24% depending on certain sensitivities. At the same time, the aggregate wealth controlled by these individuals also decreased by $15.8 trillion, or 14%, with a projected loss range of 9%-24% (Exhibit 1.3). Notably, this is the first time in nearly a decade that the ranks of the high-net-worth have gotten smaller rather than larger year-over-year.

EXHIBIT 1.2:

# The Number of Financial Elite

| Estimate | 2007 | 2010 |
|---|---|---|
| Low-end estimate | 742,000 | 564,000 |
| Best estimate | 916,000 | 751,000 |
| High-end estimate | 1,358,000 | 1,209,000 |

EXHIBIT 1.3:

# Aggregate Wealth Controlled by the Financial Elite*

| Estimate | 2007 (in US$ trillions) | 2010 (in US$ trillions) |
|---|---|---|
| Low-end estimate | $84.3 | $63.8 |
| Best estimate | $112.6 | $96.8 |
| High-end estimate | $141.9 | $129.1 |

*For methodological purposes, the amount of private wealth per affluent family was capped at US$2.4 billion.*

The bad news is that the financial elite is a shrinking group with less wealth to manage, which means competition for their business will intensify, and those that remain are surely still coping with the aftereffects of the losses and seeking ways to recapture their wealth. The good news is that it's still a sizable population who's members both want and need the guidance of wealth managers and professional advisors—and may be more open to new ideas, new approaches and new professionals than ever before.

We'll offer you a final reminder: Although these estimates are well-constructed and thoughtful, they are subject to the effects of changing asset values, the state of the economy and the entrepreneurial drive of the wealthy.

In the next chapter, we discuss how people join the ranks of the financial elite and the methods that are most common and most effective.

# The Roads to Riches

There are many ways—both legal and illegal—to become wealthy and the more you know about a person's route to affluence the better you will understand his or her mindset, risk tolerances and other perspectives on money, relationships and lifestyle. In this chapter, we'll discuss several methods of procuring wealth and the relative effectiveness of each.

## MARRYING FOR MONEY

Perhaps the most fascinating way to get rich is through marriage. And while there are many high-profile, and successful, examples of this technique regularly on display in the tabloids our research shows that most people approach the opportunity with a highly personalized point-of-view that translates into undersized goals and disappointing results.

In a national survey we spoke with almost 1,000 unmarried people with average annual incomes ranging from US$30,000 to US$60,000 (Exhibit 2.1). The majority of people recognize that money can ease a lot of concerns and "marrying up" makes perfect sense provided the circumstances are acceptable. About two-thirds of our survey respondents expressed a high degree of interest in marrying someone for their money, and the associated fiscal security, if that person was "likable" and "not ugly" (Exhibit 2.2). Proportionately more women than men reported being amenable to the idea, though one female respondent explained the inverse relationship between looks and wealth by stating "the uglier he is, the more money he has to have."

**EXHIBIT 2.1:**

# Unmarried Individuals

N = 956 Individuals

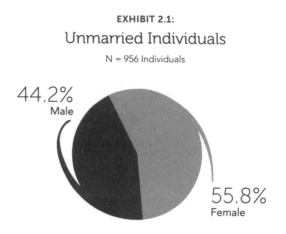

44.2%
Male

55.8%
Female

**EXHIBIT 2.2:**

# "Very" or "Extremely" Willing to Marry for Money

N = 956 Individuals

72.8%
Female

65.1%
Weighted
Average

55.3%
Male

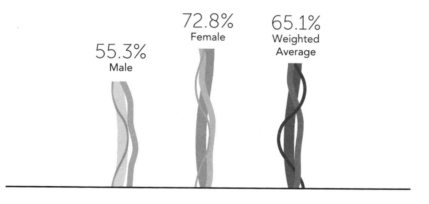

Though the value of a dollar has declined significantly in recent years, it turns out that US$1 million is still a magic number for many. When queried about the amount of money it would take to seal the deal, every respondent gave a figure that exceeded US$1 million—in some cases, however, not by much. Men said it would take an average US$1.1 million to consider marrying someone they didn't love, while women set their sights nearly four times higher at US$3.8 million to take the plunge (Exhibit 2.3).

**EXHIBIT 2.3:**
# Amount of Money Required (in US$ millions)
N = 623 Individuals

$3.8
Female

$2.7
Weighted
Average

$1.1
Male

As this research illustrates, most people define wealth in terms that don't approach the levels of the financial elite. Instead, they think about it in the context of their personal situation, income and experience. The average of US$2.7 million cited by our survey respondents is a far cry from the monies they would need to be considered part of the financial elite, not to mention the myriad drawbacks of marrying someone solely for their financial resources.

## HITTING THE FINANCIAL JACKPOT

As mentioned previously, there are a lot of ways to get rich—and then there are the proven ways of navigating to the top of the financial pyramid. The six principal kinds of wealth generation are:

- **Equity wealth.** Throughout the world, equity wealth is the most common route to affluence. This is wealth created by having an equity stake in an ongoing successful enterprise. Very often these enterprises are formal businesses, however they can also be commission-based activities, intellectual property and the like.

- **Post-equity wealth.** This kind of wealth is created when the owner of the "enterprise" sells his or her stake to another person or company and subsequently gets rich (or richer). Equity stakes are often illiquid assets, so many people only realize their private wealth once the sales transaction is complete.

- **Corporate wealth.** Senior officers in public and private corporations have amassed sizable estates from handsome compensation packages including bonuses, deferred compensation, restricted stock and stock options. It's important to note that this form of wealth is strongly correlated with performance of the world equity markets and the state of global economies.

- **Inherited wealth.** "Trust babies" of all ages are the benefactors of someone else's success and inheritances, and while captivating, are relatively rare. In fact, inherited wealth represents less than 10% of all private wealth.

- **Illegal wealth.** Either in the form of criminal activities or flight capital, illegal wealth is extensive and extreme. Worth noting, however, is that the wealth of most successful criminals is derived from their equity ownership of an illicit enterprise.

- **Fortuitous wealth.** The least likely and least predictable way of getting rich is by getting lucky, say by winning the lottery or finding an abandoned Van Gogh painting at the side of the road.

## EQUITY REIGNS

Having a stake in a successful enterprise is the most likely way to become wealthy and this is especially true when you consider the financial elite. As evidence, we identified the principal source of wealth for a group of private jet owners (individuals with an average net worth of US$89 million and an average annual income of US$9 million) and for the families who established single-family offices.

Three-quarters of private jet owners derived their fortunes from equity or post-equity wealth (Exhibit 2.4). The remaining quarter created their fortunes from high-level corporate positions, as celebrities (many of whom have business ventures as well) and through inheritances. Even when business success does not convert to these astronomical levels of wealth, business success does indeed prove to be the route to great affluence.

**EXHIBIT 2.4:**

# Source of Jet Owner Wealth

N = 661 Jet Owners | Source: *The Sky's the Limit: Marketing Luxury to the New Jet Set* (2007)

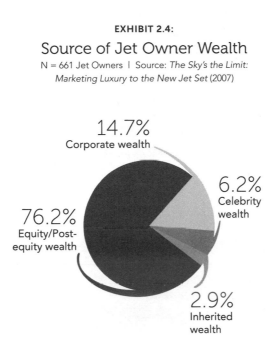

14.7%
Corporate wealth

6.2%
Celebrity wealth

76.2%
Equity/Post-equity wealth

2.9%
Inherited wealth

The source of wealth among the single-family offices in our survey was overwhelmingly equity or post-equity related wealth (Exhibit 2.5). Nine out of every ten family fortunes, whether it's the second or third generation who is presently in control, is directly tied to having a "piece of the action."

**EXHIBIT 2.5:**

# Underlying Source of Wealth for Single-Family Offices

N = 376 Single-Family Offices

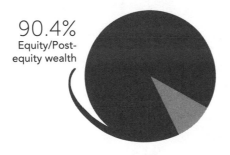

90.4%
Equity/Post-equity wealth

What's clear is that the route to extreme wealth typically revolves around the ownership and transference—or buying and selling—of assets. While having an equity position that translates into wealth is generally critical, it takes a very special person to make it all happen and to create a considerable fortune. In fact, we've repeatedly discerned that the self-made financial elite think, and, more importantly, act differently than those who are less affluent and this mindset and pattern of behavior is generally more pronounced as the level of wealth increases. We refer to these characteristics or "rules of conduct" that dramatically increase a person's ability to join the financial elite (and, potentially, become a self-made billionaire) as *Money Rules.*

In the next chapter we explore the seven rules followed by the world's wealthiest individuals and how those differ from the attitudes and actions of emerging wealth.

# Money Rules

There are some niche insights gained as a result of a career spent studying and working with the high-net-worth and ultra-high net-worth markets. The most obvious is an innate understanding of core demographics—things like age, education, gender and net worth—and to what extent those factor into the priorities, concerns and lifestyle choices of the affluent. Knowing that someone is self-made rather than the recipient of an inheritance, for instance, can reveal a lot about their approach to finances and family. In fact, the higher a person's net worth the greater the likelihood they generated all, or much of it, themselves. And, as discussed in the previous chapter, our research repeatedly shows that equity ownership is the most common source of wealth among the ultra-affluent.

A less obvious learning, but equally insightful, is an understanding of psycho-graphics—the motivations, mindsets and attitudes—that separate the affluent from their less wealthy counterparts, and how those translate into practiced behaviors and personal responses. As with demographics, we've been able to identify common psychological attributes and behaviors among the financial elite, and just as we know that equity ownership is behind the large majority of significant wealth, so too are these core actions and mindsets.

Over the past decade, Prince & Associates, Inc. has pioneered the ethnographic study of wealth-generating behaviors in the context of billionaires and those on the fast-track to billionaire status. Along the way, we extracted some specific learnings that are applicable to less wealthy individuals and even certain pockets of the mass population. Together, these seven approaches can be seen as a set of rules (a code of conduct, if you will) that are often followed rigorously by the super-rich and ultimately result in huge fortunes.

To reach the apex of the financial pyramid tends to require a tremendous commitment to the Money Rules. For our select few clients whom we believe to be capable and committed (see *Chapter 14: Turnarounds and Lift-offs*), we construct highly customized Personal Wealth Creation Programs. Following this collaborative process, we stay by their sides helping them turn their financial dreams into golden realities.

While we're quite particular in providing this expertise at a very intense and high-touch level, we nevertheless have provided the methodology in other venues to a wide variety of affluent entrepreneurs of all stripes from hedge fund managers and business owners to celebrities and professionals. Each and every one of them wanted to be significantly more monetarily successful. Even if the person does not want to go especially deep with respect to the Money Rules, the adroit implementation of these "rules of conduct" can readily provide the path up the financial pyramid even though their monetary goals are short of the very top.

# SEVEN RULES OF CONDUCT

What follows are a number of the critical Money Rules that are at the core of each affluent and successful client's Personal Wealth Creation Program:

> #1. Commit to extreme wealth.
>
> #2. Engage in enlightened self-interest.
>
> #3. Put yourself in the line of money.
>
> #4. Pay everyone involved.
>
> #5. Connect for profit and results.
>
> #6. Use failure to improve and refocus.
>
> #7. Stay highly centered.

While the Money Rules work best in concert, for purposes of simplicity and brevity, let's review these "rules of conduct" individually in greater detail.

# #1. COMMIT TO EXTREME WEALTH

Truth be told, many people would like to be rich but haven't committed the time or effort necessary to get there. Doing so can often mean being faced with choices that help you reach your goal of being wealthy at the expense of something else that may be important to you. Following this rule means having a clear sense that money is your most critical objective and, by doing so, consciously prioritizing activities with the highest potential return and assigning a lower priority to most everything else in your life.

Most people, while wanting to be very wealthy, are not willing to do what it takes to achieve such financial success. They're more talk than action. When it comes right down to it, they're not willing to do what it takes to create extreme wealth. A question we always ask of perspective clients is: "What are you NOT willing to do?"

# #2. ENGAGE IN ENLIGHTENED SELF-INTEREST

Today's society praises caring, compromise and collaboration as a way to find the common ground where people (or institutions) with different goals and vantage points can realize enough of their goals to be satisfied. While the approach is comfortable, especially for those who abhor confrontation, it is the anathema of most ambitious and successful people. The wealthiest among us are focused on reaching their specific goals and never waver or allow themselves to be derailed by the chance for group happiness or pleas for fairness and justice. Simultaneously, following this rule means doing the advance work necessary to handle any turn of events, to create an unfair advantage, or exploit the weakness in an opponent.

Operationally, enlightened self-interest takes many forms. One example of this behavior pattern is evidenced during negotiations. Skilled negotiation is at the heart of successful economic endeavors. As Bill Gates said, "In business, you don't get what you deserve, but only what you negotiate."

# #3. PUT YOURSELF IN THE LINE OF MONEY

Simply put, some endeavors are more fruitful and rewarding than others. For instance, working on Wall Street is typically more lucrative than social work and being your own boss gives you a greater chance for wealth than working for somebody else. Since most skills are portable, it only makes sense that the super-rich apply theirs in the situations that offer the highest pay-backs. Following this rule means pursuing the fields and initiatives that have the highest potential for outsize returns, now and in the future.

Often a key aspect of being in the "line of money" is having "a piece of the action." As empirically verified by the research cited in the previous chapter, the self-made super-rich tend to have equity stakes in enterprises that, they conclude, are likely to make them wealthier. The multiplier effect of these equity stakes is what generates the significantly above-average returns.

# #4. PAY EVERYONE INVOLVED

The exceedingly wealthy assume everyone has a degree of self-interest that can be used to their advantage and they target that nature in others when building a team around themselves. They never assume people are willing to work for satisfaction or fulfillment, and therefore reward handsomely—with cash, equity or some other form of currency—in an effort to cultivate the loyalty and specific behaviors in their colleagues that can help them advance toward their long-term goals.

The big question is what to pay people—how much? The answer is predicated on Value Determination (see below). This becomes all the more the case when the super-rich are using "social currency." For meaningful and ongoing success, it's critical that all the people involved feel they're being treated fairly.

# #5. CONNECT FOR PROFIT AND RESULTS

Highly successful people think about networking as a means to an end—finding the person, the information or the tools that gets them one step closer to their personal and professional objectives. Following this rule means maintaining a small but deep network of relationships that lead not to friendship but to power and influence. This form of nodal networking maximizes the time and effort spent toward realizing profit and identifying those things that can further enhance your profit.

Nodal networking is where a person has a few very powerful, highly targeted, deep relationships who in turn have an array of similar relationships of their own. This form of networking enables the super-rich to maximize their time and efforts as they connect for profit, first indirectly then directly, with a wide variety of people that can make them wealthier.

# #6. USE FAILURE TO IMPROVE AND REFOCUS

Failure is inevitable, so most of the super-rich don't worry about avoiding it. Instead they focus on learning from each experience and using the lessons to get an advantage the next time around. Rather than obsessing about lost opportunities and getting discouraged, you should study your failures and do all you can to prevent repeating missteps.

Central to "using" failure is perseverance. When confronted by personal or professional disasters, the super-rich express a powerful determination of will and keep going. Amusingly, when it comes to this issue, many of the super-rich quote Nietzche who said, "What doesn't kill us makes us stronger." In effect, failure energizes these people to achieve.

# #7. STAY HIGHLY CENTERED

The wealthiest among us know there are very few things they do well, what they want to achieve and what role they play in generating wealth. Being highly centered means sticking to your plan and not getting distracted by other opportunities or events that call for new and different skill sets. The super-rich are exceptionally capable of focusing themselves and delegating to others in a way that leaves little room for derailment or doubt.

The self-made super-rich concentrate their efforts on those few things and do everything in their power to delegate other tasks and activities to others. The importance of being centered is so critical to business success and private wealth creation that we address the topic in the next section.

A good way to understand the power and purpose of these rules is to compare them to the typical approach of a successful business professional or Middle-Class Millionaire, someone with emerging wealth but not yet a member of the financial elite (Exhibit 3.1). As you'll see, the behaviors that are considered acceptable in most social or professional environments are designed to promote harmony and mutually beneficial outcomes, rather than substantial wealth or clear winners.

**EXHIBIT 3.1:**

## Comparative Approaches to Wealth Creation

| Rule | Professional | Super-Rich |
|------|-------------|------------|
| Commitment | Seek work/life balance, where money is only one piece of the equation | Creating wealth is regularly the top priority and overarching motivation |
| Self-Interest | Looking to make everyone "happy" or get a fair deal | Making sure they are winners, strategically or financially, in every meaningful situation |
| Line of Money | Believes in doing what they love and the money will follow | Pursue only those activities that have significant probability of generating above-average financial returns |
| Connections | Network with a lot of people for social, cultural and business purposes | Build strong relationships with a handful of strategically valuable people |
| Payouts | Create rapport and look to help others | Ensure each party is duly compensated for his or her contribution |
| Failure | Failure is a major obstacle that can cause setbacks, reassessments and new directions | Failure is a learning experience and a motivator |
| Centered | Concentrate on overcoming weaknesses and becoming a well-rounded person | Concentrate on a very few, especially strong and appropriate, strengths and delegate everything else |

In essence, these rules are a form of shorthand that often explains the personal and professional goals of an ultra-affluent person. They can have a bearing on his or her priorities for family offices services and should be thought of as a blueprint for wealth creation expertise. Another way to think about the rules is how they can be applied in the context of a particular individual. The seven rules described above have become the core premise of certain one-on-one consulting we do with successful professionals, entrepreneurs and other members of the financial elite seeking to amass greater fortunes. In the course of these engagements we help each person develop and implement a Personal Wealth Creation Program to systematize the rules and create methodologies for mastering and regularly deploying them in ways that best fit their skills and objectives.

For this discussion, the point is that the empirical work we've done coupled with an ethological approach studying the self-made super-rich clearly shows the path to the pinnacle of the financial pyramid. To get a better feel, let's consider some of the empirical evidence validating the highly centered rule as being instrumental to creating extreme wealth.

# BEING HIGHLY CENTERED

Being highly centered is characteristic of the most successful and wealthiest individuals. By "highly centered" we mean that they are clear about their extraordinary skills and talents and how to best leverage them toward a specific set of intermediary goals with the end result being extreme wealth.

Central to being highly centered is an understanding by these individuals as to what they're very good at—their unique skills and talents—and what they're not the best at. Moreover, the super-rich not only understand this but they're able to capitalize on it. What's evident is that being highly centered dramatically influences greater private wealth. Over the years, we've looked at various affluent segments and discovered the power of being highly centered. Here, we'll review some of those findings. Let's consider celebrities and affluent family business owners. Let's also look at small business owners to see that being highly centered is critical to meaningful personal wealth at every level of affluence.

## CELEBRITIES

Unfortunately, very few celebrities can be described as highly centered and this has a direct correlation to their emotional satisfaction and career success. Just 22% of celebrities evaluated are considered highly centered, with the other 78% much less so (Exhibit 3.2).

**EXHIBIT 3.2:**

# Degree of Centeredness
# Among Celebrities

N = 1,015 celebrities (based on 203 entertainment attorneys)
Source: *Fame & Fortune: Maximizing Celebrity Wealth* (2008)

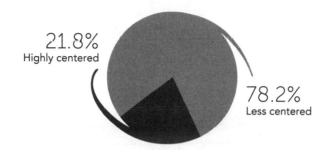

**21.8%**
Highly centered

**78.2%**
Less centered

For celebrities, being highly centered has numerous advantages that can increase the overall quality of life. One of those advantages is greater wealth; celebrities that were highly centered had significantly greater average net worth than those that were less centered (Exhibit 3.3). And when viewed on a median basis, highly centered celebrities had roughly twice the total assets. Without question, a larger bank account can be a nice byproduct of a centered approach.

**EXHIBIT 3.3:**

# Celebrity Net Worth by Centeredness
# (in US$ millions)

N = 1,015 celebrities (based on 203 entertainment attorneys)
Source: *Fame & Fortune: Maximizing Celebrity Wealth* (2008)

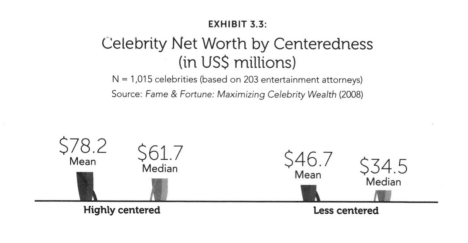

**$78.2**
Mean

**$61.7**
Median

**$46.7**
Mean

**$34.5**
Median

**Highly centered**

**Less centered**

## AFFLUENT FAMILY BUSINESS OWNERS.

In a survey of 242 affluent business owners (mean value of the business = US$731.3 million), we found that less than one-third were highly centered (Exhibit 3.4).

EXHIBIT 3.4:

## Degree of Centeredness Among
## Affluent Family Business Owners

N = 242 Affluent Family Business Owners | Source: *Protecting the Family Fortune: Advanced Planning for Ultra-High-Net-Worth Family Businesses and Their Owners* (2008)

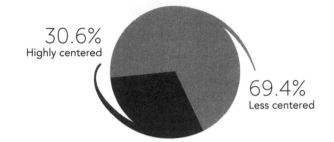

**30.6%**
Highly centered

**69.4%**
Less centered

What we found is that the highly centered affluent family business owners were 6.2 times more personally wealthy than those who are less centered. So, for every US$1 million a less centered affluent family business owner is worth, the highly centered affluent family business owner is worth US$6.2 million (Exhibit 3.5).

**EXHIBIT 3.5:**

## Comparative Wealth by Centeredness Among Affluent
## Family Business Owners (in US$ millions)

N = 242 Affluent Family Business Owners | Source: *Protecting the Family Fortune: Advanced Planning for Ultra-High-Net-Worth Family Businesses and Their Owners* (2008)

**$6.2**
Highly centered

**$1.0**
Less centered

## SMALL BUSINESS OWNERS

In a survey of 1,402 small business owners, about three-quarters of them have a net worth (including the equity in their businesses) of less then US$10 million. Almost a fifth of the business owners have a net worth between US$10 million and US$20 million. And, the remaining business owners have a net worth greater than US$20 million (Exhibit 3.6).

**EXHIBIT 3.6:**

# Business Owner Net Worths

N = 1,402 Business Owners

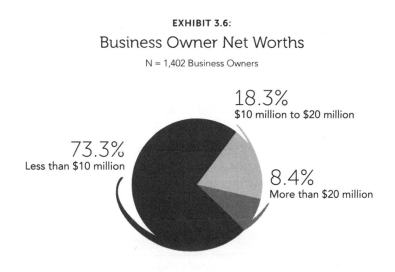

**18.3%**
$10 million to $20 million

**73.3%**
Less than $10 million

**8.4%**
More than $20 million

By statistically controlling factors, such as the age of the business, the type of business, the capital structure and so forth, we were able to determine the impact of being highly centered to creating private wealth. As we see in Exhibit 3.7, the wealthier business owners are proportionately more highly centered.

**EXHIBIT 3.7:**

# Percentage Who Are Highly Centered

N = 1,402 Business Owners

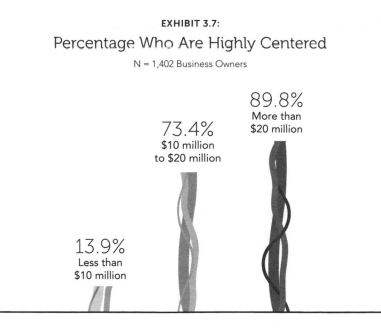

**89.8%**
More than
$20 million

**73.4%**
$10 million
to $20 million

**13.9%**
Less than
$10 million

# TOOLS, TECHNIQUES AND PROCESSES

Turning back to the billionaires and those who are fast-tracking to the top of the financial pyramid and combining these insights with a need to systematize what they do often instinctively, we've developed and refined an array of tools, techniques and processes that can be instrumental in creating extreme wealth. Included here are:

- **Noncompetitive mixed-strategies game theory.** The intent is to think strategically and insightfully about the competition as well as about supporters. By understanding how each party will act in each situation a competitive advantage is gained.

- **Pro formas per decision.** This is also referred to as "running the numbers." An informed decision cannot be made until there's a determination of the costs and returns. People tend to get so wrapped up with the "obvious success" of some business venture that they fail to see the hurdles and landmines in the road.

- **Profiling.** Developing an in-depth understanding of other people that can be helpful in creating extreme wealth requires proactively and methodically profiling them. The profiling process is a meticulous well-developed system for understanding their motivations, recognizing their limitations and developing socio-diagrams of their networks.

- **Egocentric mapping.** As noted, it proves very useful to map out the nodal and broader networks. In this particular socio-diagram, the starting point is the individual—hence, egocentric. However, just depicting the relationships with measures such as frequency of contact, intensity of interactions and their linking abilities is insufficient. With this tool, we incorporate an overlay grid that details how each of these people can provide a supporting role (or not) in each initiative.

- **Value determination.** If it's essential to compensate everyone for their contributions—and it is—then there has to be a systematic way to determine the value they provide. This process is derivative of the Delphi approach. While this methodology provides us with a solid starting point, the power of the process is our conjoint ability to ascertain the minimum payout required to achieve the desired results.

# THE "MAGIC" OF THE MONEY RULES

As consultants helping the rich become super-rich and sometimes the super-rich become many times wealthier, there's the mistaken idea that we possess some sort of secret knowledge, some magic. For instance, by providing direction and insights to the high-end of the super-rich on how to better approach certain professional situations or better leverage their relationships for pecuniary gain, we're oft times given greater credit for their considerable financial accomplishments then we deserve. The effectiveness of the Personal Wealth Creation Programs we conceptualize and execute in concert with our super-rich clients is more a credit to them than to us.

When we've worked with the once super-rich to strategically leverage their relationships, resources and talents resulting in them becoming super-rich again, or for the mildly very, very wealthy to fast-tack to super-rich status (see *Chapter 14: Turnarounds & Lift-offs*), we're given much too much praise for their financial rebound or their exponential acceleration to extreme wealth. All in all, we admittedly find it humorous when we're seen by people enormously more economically successful and talented than we are as possessing some secret knowledge on how to become extremely wealthy.

Let's be totally transparent. There is no secret knowledge. There are no magic runes, no alchemic formulas, no transformational rituals that result in extreme wealth. Being one with the universe, thinking positive, speaking victories, visualizing the preferred state, studying the ancient grimoires (and we have an extensive collection of such arcane tomes) will not make someone extremely wealthy.

All we have done is apply academic rigor to identifying the mindset and behavioral patterns that produce extreme wealth. In addition, we're adept consultants to the super-rich when it comes to private wealth creation and wealth preservation. If we can be credited with anything, we have systematized these "rules of conduct" and developed effective pedagogical methodologies for mastering them. We can also be credited with being able to work closely with the super-rich to keep the process of creating extreme wealth tightly "on track." In other words, we developed and continually refine the Personal Wealth Creation Program methodology. It's an array of interconnected insights, processes and actions—tools and techniques—that we continue to perfect.

# The Angel Investor

# The Angel Investor

By Russ Alan Prince and Hannah Shaw Grove

*Walking into his apartment—three floors in all—is like walking into a 17th century manor house. The impression is created by the décor of the place such as the paintings adorning the walls and the floor to ceiling collection of rare books in the library. The anomaly is the home office where technology reigns.*

He's an investor—an angel investor to be precise. He runs an investment consortium comprised of wealthy private investors including a few single-family offices. Each deal is a stand-alone. He's responsible for putting the deals together from beginning to end. For this, he receives 20% off the top before the remaining profit is split proportionately among the investors.

The consortium only invests in new software. He has a person managing a team of finders. The finders identify the opportunities and if a deal is struck they receive a modest flat fee. As he explained it, the finders dredge the hacker conventions, Internet chat rooms and the like for "geeks" who have written interesting software. What's telling is that 80% to 90% of the innovators they find come to them by word of mouth. Because of the success of the innovators who work with the angel investor, these inno-vators aggressively refer their peers.

Most of these innovators are seriously interested in ways to profit from their software but don't know how. He gets excited when they identify an innovator that uses a hacker handle instead of his real name. He sees this as an indicator of a fascination with technology, a strong association with a particular sub-culture and—most telling—limited business acumen.

The opportunities the consortium are interested in are new software that are mildly additive—a small step ahead—of existing already commercialized software. He explains that they're not looking for home runs, triples or even doubles. He just wants a steady stream of singles. Nevertheless, because of the way he structures the deals each single is a financial double or triple for him and his fellow investors. More to the point, for every dollar they invest, on average, they make back two or three dollars, usually within two years. The consortium does not concern itself with long-term investments. On the contrary, they see themselves as software company flippers.

By the traditional definition, he and his fellow investors are somewhat unorthodox angel investors. As the night progresses and the cognac flows, we find that he is an angel investor with horns.

## *A Predator with a Halo*

Let's begin by recognizing that our angel investor is not interested in much more than growing his sizeable personal fortune. As such, he's not enamored by or even interested in technology. He understands almost nothing of what he invests in. For him, his methodology is merely a means for him to further line his pockets. What's also clear is that he realizes the way to extreme wealth is not in innovation.

Innovation is expensive and risky. He looks at long-term innovation as a luxury that is costly to protect and monetize. The most successful business people take the brainchildren of innovators and convert them into wealth. These people are entrepreneurs not technologists. They couldn't possibly be successful if they spent all their time writing code, for instance.

What we found so interesting is his disdain for innovators. He pointed out the inventors who spend hundreds of years trying to create an ornithopter. When people talk about the new paradigm or thinking outside the box, he says he smiles. As his interest is on growing his personal fortune, he understands that capitalizing on what's commercially viable is superior to thinking of an innovation that still must be adroitly brought to market. He points out that Bill Gates did not originally develop DOS. He acquired it and as a shrewd businessman he monetized the opportunity.

The angel investor has carefully evaluated the returns on software innovations and concluded the answer lies in first acquiring the rights to the innovations and then quickly selling those rights to a hungry buyer. He explains that he aims to profit from the creativity of others. After listening to his stories of the firms he invested in and the results he achieved, we were able to deconstruct his approach. It proves to be quite simple.

The first step is to find an innovation that is a small, but important, step ahead of a commercial product. This concurrently specifies the potential buyers of the software innovation. If these conditions are met, the angel investor structures a deal with the innovators. These deals tend to strongly favor the angel investor. Many times, for instance, the consortium is able to switch out their capital for a bank loan while retaining the same equity in the venture. When they make this transition, the innovators regularly have to provide a personal guarantee, but not the investors. In all their investments, the angel investor determines the fate of the innovation which is always a quick sale.

The angel investor has unearthed a potentially profitable situation where the parties involved cannot get out of their own way. Before he makes a deal with the innovators, he calls in his evaluation team. There's a lot of financial analysis, but that's a small part of the decision to invest. These types of deals—especially predicated on flipping—are about the people involved. The personalities and orientations of the innovators and the corporate executives are the key factors. Hence, the angel investor develops in-depth files on the respective parties often with the assistance of world-class investigators.

If the stars align, he sprinkles a little money into the mix and exits with a lot more money. No matter what, he cannot lose money—the downside is completely covered. When he takes his leave, everyone feels good—even if he and his fellow investors are the ones with most and, once in a while, all the money.

## Everybody Wins

The angel investor is expertly choreographing these deals and he with his fellow investors are pretty much making all the money, yet everybody comes out a winner. What happens is that the angel investor works very hard to make certain that each person's expectations are being well managed. From the beginning he understands the needs and wants of all the parties involved. Consequently, he spends the time and effort necessary to ensure each person clearly understands what's possible as well as the limitations.

As for our angel investor... he wins big as does the consortium. For him, it's not about risk taking. He takes very little risk. His focus is not on the upside but on the downside. His investment decisions are made based entirely on personal pro formas. As we noted, he has no interest in the software per se. What he searches for are vulnerabilities in people—the innovators and corporate executives—that can be exploited. Consequently, he walks away from every deal with a profit. Most times those profits are quite sizeable, sometimes not—but, so far, there's always been a profit.

# PART II

# The Family Office Today

# The Appeal of
# the Family Office

There's a certain aura surrounding the family office concept and, more than ever, the financial elite is finding the idea of single-family offices and multi-family offices extremely appealing. As evidence, there's an increasing interest among the ultra-high-net-worth in setting up their own single-family office and an even stronger interest in working with a multi-family office. While the research discussed in this chapter has some limitations due to sample size and construction (see *Appendix E: Sampling Methodology*), it's indicative of the appeal of the family office and the power of the associated business and service model.

## THE RAREFIED AIR

Over the last two decades, we've repeatedly surveyed the wealthy with respect to their attitudes, behaviors and preferences in a variety of fields including financial services, luxury acquisition and family security. In the first quarter of 2009 we spoke with approximately 100 private jet owners and one of the topics for discussion was family offices. To be included in the survey, the jet owners had to have a minimum net worth of US$30 million (Exhibit 4.1), however, the survey participants proved to be wealthier. The average net worth was US$116 million and the median net worth was US$59 million.

**EXHIBIT 4.1:**

# Net Worth of Jet Owners (in US$ millions)

N = 108 Jet Owners

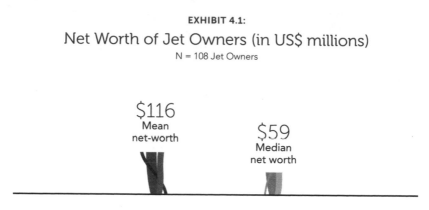

$116
Mean
net-worth

$59
Median
net worth

Less than 10% of the jet owners have a single-family office today (Exhibit 4.2). At the same time, more than twice as many are very interested in potentially creating their own SFO (Exhibit 4.3). Overall, considering the percentages noted, these results show a growing interest among the very wealthy in the single-family office concept.

**EXHIBIT 4.2:**

# Have a Single-Family Office

N = 108 Jet Owners

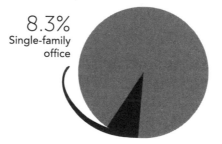

8.3%
Single-family
office

**EXHIBIT 4.3:**

# Very Interested in Establishing a Single-Family Office

N = 99 Jet Owners

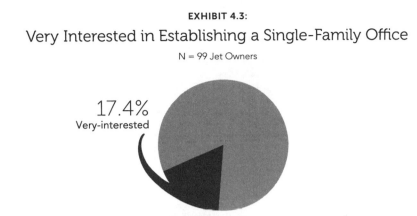

17.4%
Very-interested

Despite the interest expressed, our experience is that even high levels of curiosity often do not translate into action. And, after detailed analyses, most of the financial elite will find that a single-family office is a less optimal choice than, say, a multi-family office or another type of private wealth management provider when objectives, service preferences and fee tolerances are considered.

Of greater appeal to the jet owners studied is the multi-family office. About one-fifth of the jet owners are presently working with a multi-family office (Exhibit 4.4). Perhaps more telling is that of the jet owners working with MFOs, nine out of ten have increased the scope of their relationship within the previous two years (Exhibit 4.5). Some examples of relationship expansion include giving the MFO a larger percentage of investable assets or asking for assistance with estate and tax matters. Of the 80% of jet owners without a family office relationship, nearly three-quarters expect to be working with an MFO in the near future (Exhibit 4.6).

**EXHIBIT 4.4:**

# Presently Working with a Multi-Family Office

N = 99 Jet Owners

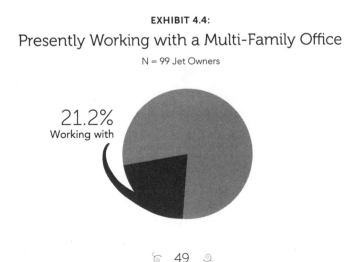

21.2%
Working with

**EXHIBIT 4.5:**

# Have Increased the Level of the Relationship in the Past 2 Years

N = 21 Jet Owners

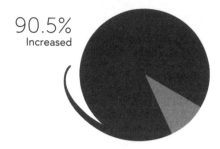

90.5%
Increased

**EXHIBIT 4.6:**

# Anticipate Working With a Multi-Family Office

N = 78 Jet Owners

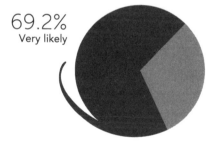

69.2%
Very likely

When we queried the jet owners about the appeal of the multi-family office, nearly all cited the highly responsive and personalized level of service (Exhibit 4.7). For 85% of the respondents, the ability of the multi-family office to provide customized solutions was critically important, followed closely by extensive financial and related expertise. About 70% are attracted by the holistic approach and somewhat fewer by the fact that the multi-family office is not pushing products.

While there are certainly other financial firms and advisors that can deliver a great service experience, provide truly customized solutions, are expert and so forth, multi-family offices are closely identified with these attributes in the mind of the high-net-worth market. This bodes well for firms that plan to reposition themselves in the vein of MFOs (see *Chapter 6: Motivations and Rationale*).

**EXHIBIT 4.7:**

## Appeal of the Multi-Family Office

N = 54 Jet Owners

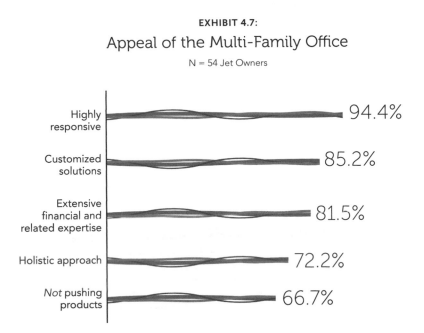

Highly responsive — 94.4%

Customized solutions — 85.2%

Extensive financial and related expertise — 81.5%

Holistic approach — 72.2%

*Not pushing products* — 66.7%

# THE MAINSTREAMING OF MULTI-FAMILY OFFICES

One of the many difficult consequences of the recent downturn is an unfortunate disconnect between high-net-worth clients and their advisory professionals. The trust that is paramount to a long-term and mutually beneficial relationship has been undermined by the chaos in the financial services industry, leaving a wake of dissatisfied and disillusioned clients looking for the value and professionalism implicit in the family office construct. In particular, MFOs have benefited from these dynamics as they offer a turnkey solution to pressing concerns and are immediately accessible to a broader group of individuals and families.

In a first-quarter 2009 survey of affluent investors (at least US$10 million in investable assets) who had moved part or all of their assets from one financial provider to another in the previous four months, MFOs were cited as the provider of choice (Exhibit 4.8). While these investors turned to a variety of organizations for assistance, they exhibited a clear bias for those that espouse the kind of service, solutions, stability and objectivity lacking in their previous relationships—and the qualities that are synonymous with family offices.

**EXHIBIT 4.8:**

# Placing Assets Taken from Primary Advisor

N = 110 Affluent Investors

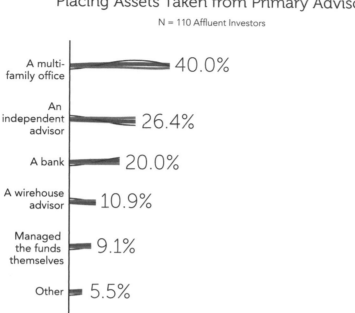

NOTE: Some respondents gave assets to more than one type of
firm causing the percentages to total more than 100%.

MFOs offer their member families a number of other attractive benefits as well. First and foremost is being part of an organization that applies its expertise across a group of people with similar wealth, priorities and challenges. There is also the immediate access to a platform of broad capabilities that can be selectively leveraged to drive a meticulous and customized planning process focused on results. Suffice it to say that the concept of the MFO holds strong interest for the financial elite (and the segments of the affluent market somewhat lower on the financial pyramid) and the research results presented above are indicative of its escalating appeal.

In the next chapter we discuss the net worth and investable assets of the families who work with SFOs and MFOs, along with the growing prominence of multi-family offices and the geographic orientation and overarching operating philosophy of today's family offices.

# Types of Family Offices

The term "family office" has a strong appeal with the connotation of significant smart money. It harkens back to the management of great fortunes and conveys a certain mystique. There has been, and continues to be, a great deal of secrecy surrounding family offices. In spite of these obstacles, we were able to conduct an intensive survey of 903 family offices using a methodology known as snowball sampling in which research participants help us identify and locate other potential participants (see *Appendix E: Sampling Methodology* for more information).

The research was conducted in the third-quarter of 2009 with the professional-in-charge at each organization. In some cases this individual surveyed was a family member and in others it was an employee of the family. The titles for the role varied as well, including everything from President to CEO to Chairman to Managing Partner. The most common title we encountered was Executive Director, which is how we refer to the role, and the research findings can be considered a proxy for today's family offices.

## DEMOGRAPHICS

Of the 903 family offices two-fifths were single-family offices and the remainder were multi-family offices (Exhibit 5.1). This segmentation proved to be critical in the way offices operate, make decisions and plan for the future and is used throughout the book.

**EXHIBIT 5.1:**

# Types

N = 903 Family Offices

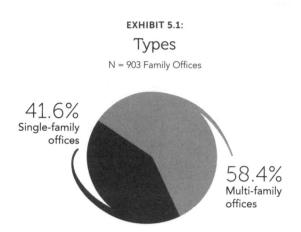

41.6%
Single-family
offices

58.4%
Multi-family
offices

Nearly 60% of the family offices had their principal location in the United States and the balance were domiciled outside the United States (Exhibit 5.2). Increasingly, private wealth is derived from businesses that cross international borders and, as a result, where a family office is domiciled is often less relevant than other aspects of how the endeavor is structured and managed.

**EXHIBIT 5.2:**

# Domicile

N = 903 Family Offices

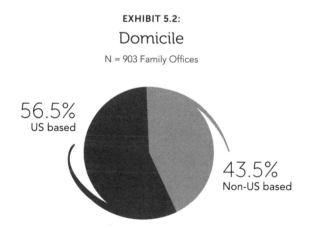

56.5%
US based

43.5%
Non-US based

A third way of analyzing this universe emerged with the use of cluster analysis, allowing us to determine the orientation of a family office relative to its attitude and approach toward wealth management. We found that family offices are either focused on the creation or preservation of wealth, with the former being more dominant (Exhibit 5.3). As the name suggests, organizations that are oriented around wealth creation have prioritized efforts that enhance or increase the fortunes of the underlying families. In contrast, entities that concentrate on wealth preservation prioritize those activities that ensure the persistence of a given family's assets. This segmentation provides an important perspective that helps families clarify their primary goals and structure their single-family office or, in the case of selecting a multi-family office, match them with the capabilities of an organization.

**EXHIBIT 5.3:**

# Orientation

N = 903 Family Offices

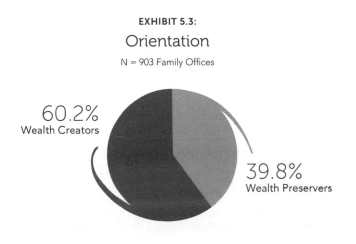

60.2%
Wealth Creators

39.8%
Wealth Preservers

## THE SINGLE-FAMILY OFFICE

Broadly speaking, an SFO is an organizational structure that manages the financial and personal affairs of one wealthy family. Because an SFO is driven purely by the needs and preferences of the underlying family, there is no standard for how one should be structured and a variety of models are in use around the globe. For instance, some SFOs are lean enterprises that focus exclusively on investing with a skeleton crew while others are robust organizations with in-house staff, numerous vendor relationships and a broad platform of services. This disparity means it was difficult to establish hard-and-fast criteria for how an SFO should be defined other than its dedication to a sole family unit. Though it remains unclear, estimates of the number of single-family offices range from a few thousand to the tens of thousands.

Moreover, for this program of research, we took liberty in including many firms we defined as single-family offices that don't "label" themselves as such. Some examples of this are:

- **A near billionaire who owns a significant operating company.** Down in the bowels of his firm is a subsidiary that, in our experience, resembles an SFO. Though he claims not to have a family office, we surveyed (with his permission) the "manager" of that subsidiary as part of our single-family office sample.

- **A wealthy family that established an investment firm specifically to manage its newly created liquid wealth.** The firm outsources all other services such as administration and tax management. Nevertheless, the firm is involved in selecting the providers and, on a scheduled basis, monitoring results. Once again, while the family did not, we defined this firm as an SFO.

- **A wealthy family with a corporate entity that provides an array of services to the family.** This company finds financial products and services for family members, but nearly everything is delivered by outside vendors. It's important to note that, unlike the two previous examples, this SFO is not providing any investment advisory services.

We encountered many similar situations in the course of our research which further reinforces that the world of SFOs is highly heterogeneous. In an effort to compile a large, exemplary survey of today's single-family offices, we were expansive in our definition of a single-family office. For instance, we have a number of organizations in our sample that do not manage investments. At the same time, this way of thinking impacts the size of the single-family office universe and, by approaching the matter as we have, we project a greater number of SFOs worldwide than do other industry authorities.

# SINGLE-FAMILY OFFICE DEMOGRAPHICS

The mean net worth of SFOs in our survey is slightly more than half a billion US dollars with a median net worth of about US$325 million (Exhibit 5.4). Investable assets equaled roughly half of net worth, with an average of about a quarter billion US dollars and a median of roughly US$125 million (Exhibit 5.5).

EXHIBIT 5.4:

## Net Worth of
## Single-Family Offices
## (in US$ millions)

N = 376 Single-Family Offices

EXHIBIT 5.5

## Investable Assets of
## Single-Family Office
## (in US$ millions)

N = 298 Single-Family Offices

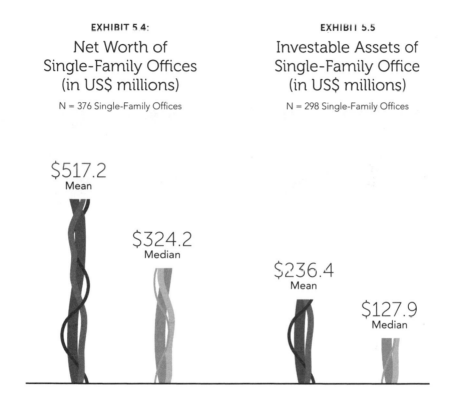

$517.2
Mean

$324.2
Median

$236.4
Mean

$127.9
Median

Outside the United States, we find the single-family offices in control of greater wealth (Exhibit 5.6). Looking at the averages, we see that non-US single-family offices oversee a net worth about 50% greater than those in the US. The median numbers are closer. With respect to investable assets, the non-US single-family offices are overseeing considerably more (Exhibit 5.7).

# Net Worth of Single-Family Offices by Domicile (in US$ millions)

N = 376 Single-Family Offices

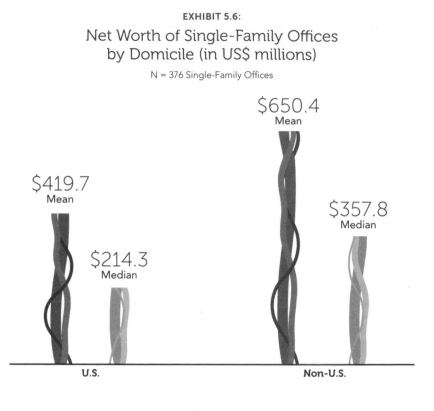

$650.4
Mean

$419.7
Mean

$357.8
Median

$214.3
Median

U.S.

Non-U.S.

# Investable Assets of Single-Family Offices by Domicile (in US$ millions)

N = 298 Single-Family Offices

$474.2
Mean

$178.6
Median

$147.5
Mean

$90.8
Median

U.S.

Non-U.S.

From the perspective of the orientation of the single-family offices, the Wealth Preservers, on average, were somewhat wealthier (Exhibit 5.8). However, they typically have about half the amount of liquid assets compared to the Wealth Creators (Exhibit 5.9).

Wealth Preservers are more affluent and their monies are less liquid. As their descriptor implies, they want to maintain their wealth. In contrast Wealth Creators are not as affluent but their monies are more liquid. They want to increase their fortunes and investing plays a crucial role in this process.

EXHIBIT 5.8:

## Net Worth of Single-Family Offices by Orientation (in US$ millions)

N = 376 Single-Family Offices

$449.4
Mean

$301.0
Median

$583.0
Mean

$346.6
Median

**Wealth Creators**          **Wealth Preservers**

EXHIBIT 5.9:

# Investable Assets of Single-Family Offices by Orientation (in US$ millions)

N = 298 Single-Family Offices

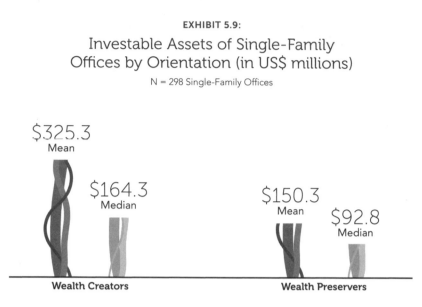

| Wealth Creators | Wealth Preservers |
|---|---|
| $325.3 Mean | $150.3 Mean |
| $164.3 Median | $92.8 Median |

## THE MULTI-FAMILY OFFICE

Conceptually, the MFO structure is an extension of the current ubiquitous wealth management model; a business that helps firms engage in fewer, deeper and more lasting relationships with affluent clients that are based on customized solutions, specialized expertise and responsive service. In reality, however, many kinds of entities identify themselves as multi-family offices creating an expansive field of disparate contenders. Though today's MFOs often come from dissimilar back-grounds—some were SFOs looking to share infrastructure costs, others were small groups of like-minded families that saw an opportunity to expand, and still others were commercial entities that chose to focus narrowly on the needs of the ultra-wealthy—now they are organizations with common attributes and are run, more often than not, with an eye toward profit and growth.

When compared to the more nebulous nature of SFOs, we were able to apply a more precise definition to MFOs. Some of this criteria includes:

- **The provision of investment advisory services.** Although we did not use this criterion with our sample of single-family offices, it was appropriate to winnow down the multitude of firms that have adopted the multi-family office moniker.

- **Clients with a minimum net worth of US$20 million and/or minimum investable assets of US$10 million.** As always, there are exceptions to the rule whether it's the children of a business owner, the best friend of a celebrity, or the mistress of a hedge fund manager and we observed a number of situations that fell outside the criteria we established due to the strategic business decisions of the MFO.

- **The regular use of the term multi-family office when describing itself.** Whereas we find quite a few single-family offices disavowing the label, the term multi-family office is being embraced with abandon (see *Appendix A: The Advisory Migration*).

# CLIENT DEMOGRAPHICS OF
# MULTI-FAMILY OFFICES

Rather than looking at the total assets under advisement at MFOs we think it's more instructional to look at how those assets are apportioned across the client base. This view allows us to get a better feel for the typical clientele and how that, in turn, informs the capabilities and day-to-day operations of the office.

In our research, the average net worth of a client at an MFO was about US$115 million and the median net worth was slightly less at approximately US$90 million (Exhibit 5.10). As with SFOs, the investable assets of clients at MFOs were roughly half of the net worth totals. The average investable assets were US$54 million and the median was US$36 million (Exhibit 5.11).

| **EXHIBIT 5.10:** | **EXHIBIT 5.11** |
|---|---|
| Net Worth of the Clients of Multi-Family Offices (in US$ millions) | Investable Assets of the Clients of Multi-Family Offices (in US$ millions) |
| N = 527 Multi-Family Offices | N = 527 Multi-Family Offices |

$116.4 Mean          $89.1 Median

$53.5 Mean          $35.9 Median

In our survey, multi-family offices domiciled outside the United States work with wealthier clients when measured by net worth (Exhibit 5.12) and investable assets (Exhibit 5.13). While many clients of multi-family offices would define themselves as global citizens, this is actually more accurate when we look at non-US domiciled multi-family offices and, as such, they are inclined to be meaningfully wealthier.

**EXHIBIT 5.12:**

## Net Worth of Clients of Multi-Family Offices by Domicile (in US$ millions)

N = 527 Multi-Family Offices

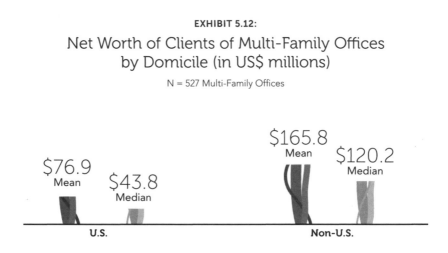

$76.9 Mean    $43.8 Median

$165.8 Mean    $120.2 Median

U.S.    Non-U.S.

**EXHIBIT 5.13:**

## Investable Assets of Clients of Multi-Family Offices by Domicile (in US$ millions)

N = 527 Multi-Family Offices

$43.8 Mean    $29.0 Median

$65.7 Mean    $44.6 Median

U.S.    Non-U.S.

As with single-family offices, the clients of Wealth Preserver multi-family offices are wealthier (Exhibit 5.14). Along the same thread of logic, the clients of Wealth Creator multi-family offices have more investable assets (Exhibit 5.15).

## Net Worth of Clients of Multi-Family Offices by Orientation (in US$ millions)

N = 527 Multi-Family Offices

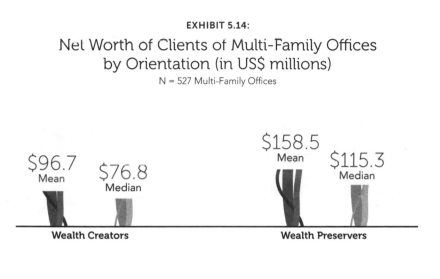

$96.7
Mean

$76.8
Median

$158.5
Mean

$115.3
Median

**Wealth Creators**        **Wealth Preservers**

## Investable Assets of Clients of Multi-Family Offices by Orientation (in US$ millions)

N = 527 Multi-Family Offices

$54.9
Mean

$41.7
Median

$41.1
Mean

$23.5
Median

**Wealth Creators**        **Wealth Preservers**

# SERVICES OF FAMILY OFFICES

Family offices, writ large, tend to provide two principal categories of services: those that relate to managing wealth and those that relate to family support (Exhibit 5.16). Under the umbrella of wealth management, our research identified investment management, advanced planning and private investment banking as the core capabilities. Simultaneously, we found that support services were either administrative or lifestyle in nature.

## EXHIBIT 5.16:

## The Array of Family Office Services

| Wealth Management | Support Services |
|---|---|
| **INVESTMENT MANAGEMENT** | **ADMINISTRATIVE** |
| Traditional asset management<br>• Asset allocation<br>• Manager selection<br>• In-house investments | Data aggregation<br>Bill paying<br>Tax preparation or coordination<br>Acting as the day-to-day CFO |
| Alternative investments<br>• Hedge funds<br>• Private equity | **LIFESTYLE** |
| **ADVANCED PLANNING** | Family security<br>Concierge Services<br>Medical Concierge |
| Estate planning<br>Asset protection planning<br>Wealth enhancement strategies | Philanthropic advisory<br>Formal family education |
| **PRIVATE INVESTMENT BANKING** | Managing fine art/collectibles<br>Property management |
| Buying and selling interests in businesses and other assets | |
| Capital raising<br>• Sourcing bank loans<br>• Sourcing investors | |

In practice, each of the sub-categories listed above is comprised of specific products (such as hedge funds or intentionally defective trusts) and services (bill paying or close protection personnel, for example) based on the needs of the underlying families. The sheer scope of possibilities and combinations mean that truly unique and thorny issues can be addressed in a wholly customized fashion without deviating from the basic operating structure. At the same time, we're seeing new types of structures emerge that are geared to the needs of niche segments of the financial elite (see *Chapter 15: Specialty Family Offices*) emphasizing the demanding and mercurial nature of this segment.

In the next chapter we examine the reasons for creating or joining a family office and the growing propensity of SFOs to consider merging with or joining an MFO.

# Motivations & Rationale

Using a statistical technique called factor analysis we were able to determine the reasons the financial elite choose to create or work with family offices (Exhibit 6.1). Overall, the primary reason is to make money, whether that is through the adroit management of personal assets or the collection of fees from a client base. Three-quarters of family offices say they want control over their personal and financial affairs and the ability to tailor the product and service offerings to better serve the needs and desires of the underlying family. Meanwhile, two-thirds see the family office as a way to achieve economies of scale in terms of pricing or vendor relationships and somewhat fewer family offices find the structure itself facilitates access to otherwise unavailable business opportunities. About half the family offices are motivated by the opportunity to leverage a proprietary platform of capabilities to attract new wealthy clients.

**EXHIBIT 6.1:**

## Motivations for Family Offices

N = 903 Family Offices

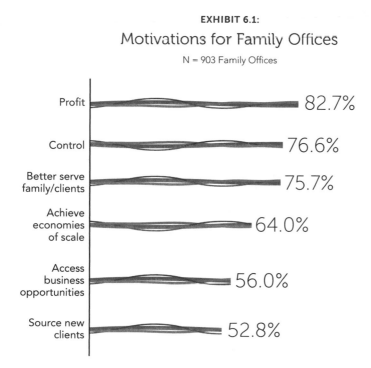

| | |
|---|---|
| Profit | 82.7% |
| Control | 76.6% |
| Better serve family/clients | 75.7% |
| Achieve economies of scale | 64.0% |
| Access business opportunities | 56.0% |
| Source new clients | 52.8% |

Although SFOs and MFOs have many similarities, their reasons for being are altogether different as evidenced by the table below (Exhibit 6.2). The primary reason for an exceedingly wealthy family to establish and maintain its own family office is control. Concurrently, for roughly two-thirds of the multi-family offices control is a primary motivation. Getting into the details, we've found that control manifests itself in the way the office is structured (including the governance and management procedures) as well as the way the wealth is invested, coordinated and transferred between family members. Furthermore, the array of services and products an SFO provides can often be tightly related to the matter of control.

Nearly all the multi-family offices are in it for the money; for them, it's a business and operated as such. For about three-fifths of the single-family offices, profit is also very important. In these cases, profit is defined as the ability to create wealth.

For about 70% of SFOs and nearly 80% of MFOs, the ability to better serve the family or wealthy clients is a significant motivator. The capacity to address a broader range of financial and related concerns in a highly consultative manner is a clear differentiator between family offices and other types of advisory firms.

About two-thirds of the respondents—relatively more single-family offices than multi-family offices—cited economies of scale as the motivation for creating and maintaining a family office. While it's possible to generate economies of scale from the various offerings that populate a family office platform, in most cases, the greatest benefits (such as institutional pricing, commission recapture and custody) are most likely derived from investment management and the associated suite of services.

About three-quarters of SFOs and two-fifths of MFOs are motivated by the ability to access otherwise unavailable business opportunities. Through the pooling of wealth, the family office has greater financial clout and, by the nature of the operation, is better positioned to identify business opportunities that would normally be out of reach or out of sight. In part, this is a function of the family's or wealthy client's personal and professional connections.

By definition, none of the single-family offices are looking for new well-heeled clients. In contrast, about nine out of ten multi-family offices are quite interested in expanding their clientele. As we saw in Chapter 4: The Appeal of the Family Office, the concept of the multi-family office is of strong interest among the financial elite and this trend can translate into meaningful growth for MFOs if pursued appropriately.

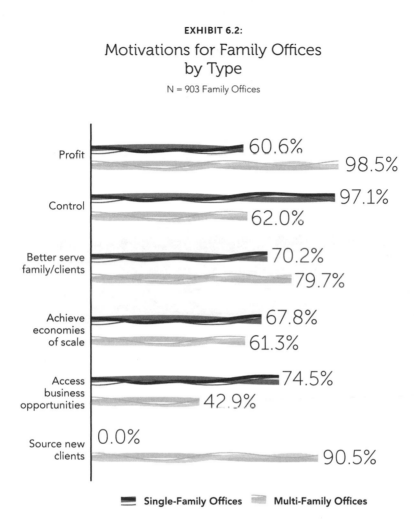

**EXHIBIT 6.2:**

## Motivations for Family Offices
## by Type

N = 903 Family Offices

| Motivation | Single-Family Offices | Multi-Family Offices |
|---|---|---|
| Profit | 60.6% | 98.5% |
| Control | 97.1% | 62.0% |
| Better serve family/clients | 70.2% | 79.7% |
| Achieve economies of scale | 67.8% | 61.3% |
| Access business opportunities | 74.5% | 42.9% |
| Source new clients | 0.0% | 90.5% |

■ **Single-Family Offices** ▬ **Multi-Family Offices**

The two biggest distinctions between the motivations of Wealth Creators and Wealth Preservers is a desire for profit and control (Exhibit 6.3). The Wealth Creators are looking to generate returns for the family office. Meanwhile, a greater percentage of Wealth Preservers are motivated by the control a family office structure can provide. To a greater degree, Wealth Creators are interested in sourcing new affluent clients than Wealth Preservers.

EXHIBIT 6.3:

# Motivations for Family Offices by Orientation

N = 903 Family Offices

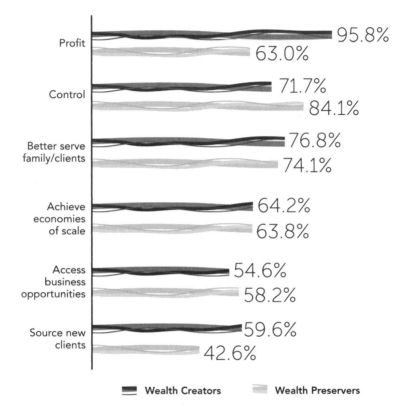

# FROM SINGLE-FAMILY OFFICE
# TO MULTI-FAMILY OFFICE

Despite the diversity of our single-family office research sample, we observed that SFOs in all their incarnations are evolving to adapt to a fast-moving and sometimes hostile environment. More and more, SFOs are becoming "structurally opportunistic." In other words, if the operational changes can deliver concrete benefits to the family they're more likely to take action. One example of this is single-family offices that have transitioned from the founders to younger generations and are consequently focusing on fewer services (see *Chapter 16: Leadership Transitions*).

The best, and most prevalent, example of these opportunistic actions are SFOs that are actively considering expansion beyond their own family to work with one or more other wealthy families, in effect transforming from an SFO to an MFO. On a related note, there are also single-family offices that are evaluating a merger with another SFO or joining an established MFO as a way to be more profitable, access a broader range of services or increase the chance of achieving their wealth management goals (Exhibit 6.4). All in all, about two-fifths of the single-family offices are exploring making one of these types of changes. A higher percentage of the Wealth Creators than the Wealth Preservers are so inclined.

**EXHIBIT 6.4:**

# "Extremely" or "Very" Interested in Becoming or
# Joining a Multi-Family Office

N = 376 Single-Family Offices

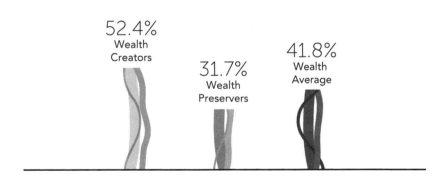

52.4%
Wealth
Creators

31.7%
Wealth
Preservers

41.8%
Wealth
Average

The primary driver behind making such a transition is profit (Exhibit 6.5). SFOs clearly see, and are attracted to, the opportunity to generate revenues by joining forces with MFOs that, in most cases, are already managed as for-profit business enterprises. For a similarly large percentage of these single-family offices, joining an MFO will allow the underlying families to be better served than they could be due to the cost constraints or limited expertise of the existing structure. The ability to distribute expenses over a larger number of families or access the resident expertise of an established MFO can result in a multitude of cost-effective opportunities for a wealthy family.

For about 60% of SFOs the chance to generate economies of scale is a key factor and for about half of them the ability to access business opportunities is a driving force. Typically, it's expected that new business and investment opportunities will come from the new wealthy families that have joined the fold and the enhanced aggregate wealth of the newly-minted MFO will make it (and its affluent clientele) eligible to participate in otherwise restricted investments and tax strategies.

**EXHIBIT 6.5:**

# Motivations for Becoming or Joining a Multi-Family Office

N = 157 Single-Family Offices

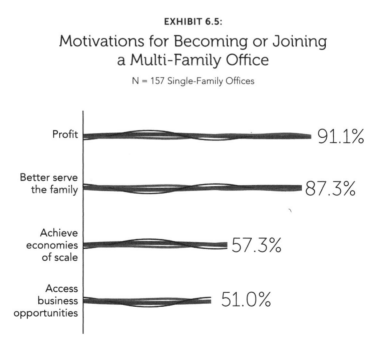

Wealth Creators, not surprisingly, are principally concerned with achieving profit or personal growth while Wealth Preservers take a more moderate view and hope to realize most of the associated benefits (Exhibit 6.6).

**EXHIBIT 6.6:**

# Motivations for Becoming or Joining
# a Multi-Family Office by Orientation

N = 157 Single-Family Offices

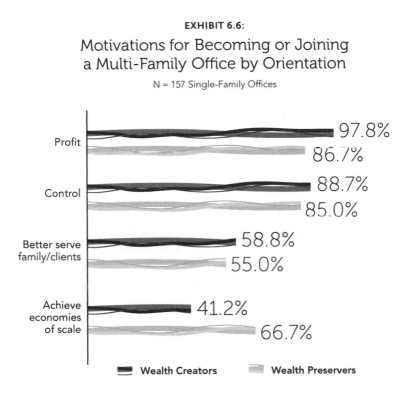

The decision to integrate one SFO into another or into an MFO is not one to be taken lightly and requires appropriate due diligence. While we know of successful transitions, they are heavily outnumbered by unsuccessful ones and attempts that were aborted once the issues came to light.

The same basic criteria that the financial elite should consider when selecting an MFO should be conceptually adopted in these situations as well (see *Appendix B: Selecting a Multi-Family Office*). And there are some additional issues that should be taken into account when contemplating the transition from SFO to MFO, such as:

- The inevitable change in operating culture.
- The necessity of more formal systems and processes.
- The potential need for new and different types of expertise.
- The change or increase in the cost and structure of personnel.
- The proactive expansion of the client base in support of growth and profits.

In the next section we examine the role of the Executive Director in the strategic and tactical operations of a family office and the essential skills of a successful leadership professional.

# *The Five Fingers*

# The Five Fingers

By Russ Alan Prince and Hannah Shaw Grove

**One finger...** *His daughter, the 22 year old with the revoked driver's license, crashed the family Maybach into a house. The car was filled with her friends in various stages of undress and surprisingly no one was wearing a seat belt. The Maybach entered the foyer, went right through the living room, made a quick visit to the den before stopping in the kitchen. No one in the car or the house was "too badly" hurt. The car converted the house into something resembling a lean-to while the car looked liked it won a demolition derby.*

The police appeared and she was arrested for driving under the influence. Everyone in the car was arrested for possession. There were three coffee cups full of ecstasy, methamphetamine and cocaine. There was also a pistol, but as one of the passengers explained, it wasn't loaded. Incidentally, the passenger was incorrect.

His daughter calls him up hysterically. He listens carefully and then makes a phone call. The person he's calling is always available, sympathetic and resourceful. He hangs up totally assured and relaxed knowing the matter will be handled properly.

The family whose house is now a tent doesn't press charges. Aside from the fact that the house was replete with numerous building violations, they are happy that they'll end up with a newly built one without any building violations. His daughter goes into rehab for alcohol abuse. Being the victim in this situation she avoids criminal charges. It turns out that the ecstasy, methamphetamine and cocaine were the property of a couple of the passengers as was the gun. Everything was taken care of with a single phone call to one of his five fingers.

*Another finger…* Every once in a while, a business deal comes along that, while problematic and potentially explosive, is a thing of beauty. He came across such a marvelous but thorny business deal. It would be a sensational coup for him but the deal had a lot of hair on it with a good possibility of turning into a large-scale train wreck.

Because of the considerable multiple downsides, the solution he conceived had two critical interconnected components. One component was a need to raise a great deal of money very, very fast. The other component was a need to gather the money without people knowing he was the driving force behind the capital raise.

He makes a phone call and the wheels of the fund raising machine are in motion. Within a couple of weeks, he has more than US$140 million sitting in one of his corporate bank accounts ready to be deployed. All the while, the capital raise and the business deal remain under the radar of his competitors and the investment banks thanks to a single phone call to one of his five fingers.

*A third finger…* Sourcing new highly qualified profitable clients proves to be the most arduous but essential part of nearly every business. Success— especially great success—is for many professionals being able to consistently garner new business.

Once every few weeks he has dinner with a "close friend." After each of these evenings out, he comes back to his office knowing a few more "perfect prospects" will be coming his way. All these prospects are certain to become clients. Everything has been deftly choreographed. All he has to do is smile and say, "Thank you" for their business—all taken care of by one of his five fingers.

## *A Very Few Very Extraordinary "Friends"*

It was at one of those perpetual parties, as the sun was just starting to rise, that he holds up his hand and spreads his fingers wide. He asks us in a slightly slurred voice what we see. Insightfully, in unison, we say a hand. He laughs and tells me we're looking at his power, the basis for his success, the reason for his fortune.

He tells us that he has five fingers—five close professionals who were instrumental in making him fabulously wealthy. His five fingers also play a very important role in keeping the darker side of the world at bay.

His five fingers don't limit him in any way from doing business with many other people. On the contrary, he has a huge database of professionals he deals with. There is however a vast difference between those relationships and the rapport he has with his five fingers. Not only is there a real chemistry between them but also there's economic super-glue that really cements their relationships. It's the trust among the people involved reinforced by a very high degree of transparency that underlie these financial agreements and makes them work so well.

## *The Beauty of the Nodal Network*

Since that day, we've discussed how his five fingers work. He loves the phrase, "never eat alone." He's very impressed at the plethora of networking events people in his business feel obligated to attend. He's delighted in the attention his competitors are giving to social networking as a way to build their practices. He points out that all these truisms and high-tech strategies are a sure and expensive road to mediocrity.

What he has is a well-developed and extensive nodal network. All he needs to do is connect with his five close relationships for they will directly or by tapping their close relationships will provide the assistance he's seeking. It doesn't matter if he needs to deal with his wayward daughter or he needs to raise hundreds of millions for a very quiet investment or he just needs a steady stream of new clients for his business.

# PART III

# The Executive Director

# Perspectives on the Position

The person in charge of a family office plays a pivotal role in its success—or lack thereof. In order to fully understand family offices, it's therefore essential to understand the role of the professional-in-charge, the level of satisfaction derived from the position and the effectiveness of standard compensation schemes. In some cases the leader of the family office is a member of an underlying family, but, in most cases, he or she is unrelated to the family and considered to be an employee. The titles for the role varied as well, including everything from President to CEO to Chairman to Managing Partner. The most common title we encountered was Executive Director, which is how we refer to the role.

## VIEWS OF THE ROLE

Nearly all the Executive Directors see themselves as critical to the effectiveness of the family office (Exhibit 7.1). We find that, for good or bad, the Executive Director is center-stage in family offices. They have the confidence of the underlying wealthy families and, as such, are making key decisions.

Although almost 60% of Executive Directors anticipate that the level of competition for their services will significantly increase, less than 6% expect to leave their jobs within the next two years. This means that the Executive Directors, in general, are not actively looking for new employment but could still be enticed by an interesting and personally rewarding offer.

**EXHIBIT 7.1:**
# Views of the Role
N = 903 Family Offices

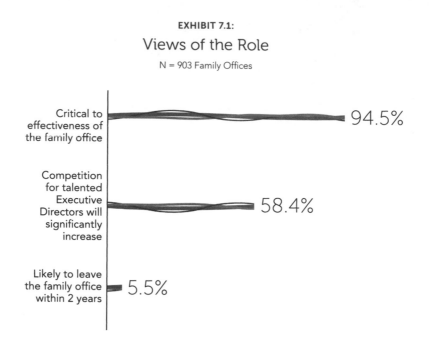

When we segment these findings by type of family office we find a dramatic difference with respect to the recruiting environment (Exhibit 7.2). While only 40% of Executive Directors in SFOs expect the demand for their skills and expertise to dramatically increase, more than 70% of the Executive Directors in MFOs anticipate a boom in opportunities. This differential can be partially attributed to the recent expansion of MFOs and their profit orientation. We can also deduce that professionals at MFOs are more easily identified and approached by recruiters as well as competitors and, therefore, receive more inquiries.

**EXHIBIT 7.2:**

# Views of the Role by Type

N = 903 Family Offices

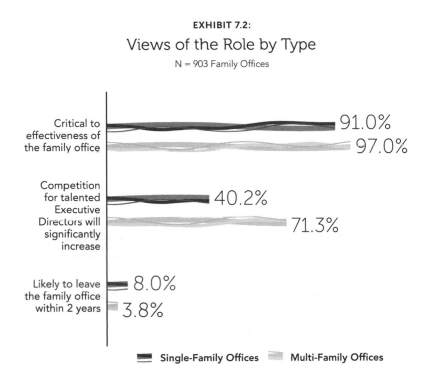

When we consider the orientation of the family offices, it is Executive Directors at Wealth Creators that are approached more frequently for new employment opportunities (Exhibit 7.3) and this is due to direct involvement in situations that translate into profits for the families and the firms. At the same time, family offices focused on wealth creation have a relatively higher profile when compared to those that focus on wealth preservation.

**EXHIBIT 7.3:**

## Views of the Role by Orientation

N = 903 Family Offices

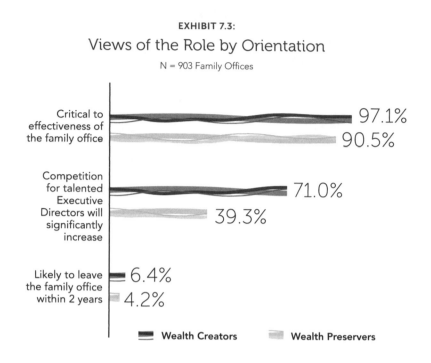

Critical to effectiveness of the family office — 97.1% / 90.5%

Competition for talented Executive Directors will significantly increase — 71.0% / 39.3%

Likely to leave the family office within 2 years — 6.4% / 4.2%

■ **Wealth Creators**    ▬ **Wealth Preservers**

## SATISFACTION CONSIDERATIONS

While very few Executive Directors are actively seeking new positions, this doesn't mean they're content with the state of their careers. Close to 65% are very or extremely satisfied with their total compensation package and slightly fewer are similarly satisfied with the scope of their responsibilities (Exhibit 7.4).

**EXHIBIT 7.4:**

## Satisfaction

N = 903 Family Offices

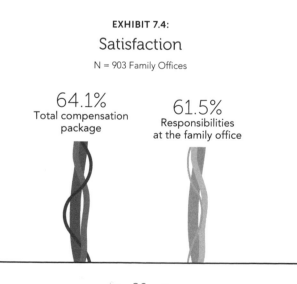

64.1%
Total compensation package

61.5%
Responsibilities at the family office

Roughly half the Executive Directors in SFOs are satisfied with their total compensation packages (Exhibit 7.5). Broadly speaking, these professionals feel they are doing better than they have in years past or in similar positions at other organizations. For more information about the 2008 earnings of these professionals (see *Appendix C: Executive Director Compensation at Single-Family Offices*). Meanwhile, proportionately more of the Executive Directors in MFOs are satisfied due largely to the pay-for-performance compensation models that articulate clear goals for employees and rewards for achieving those goals. In our experience, MFOs that employ pay-for-performance schemes typically have more satisfied employees (and Executive Directors) than the family offices that do not.

**EXHIBIT 7.5:**

# Satisfaction by Type

N = 903 Family Offices

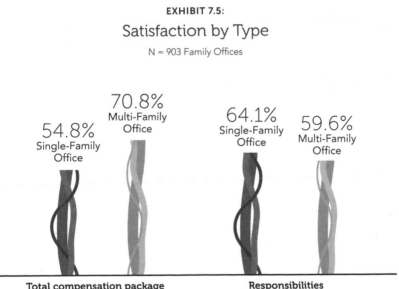

| Total compensation package | Responsibilities at the family office |
|---|---|

A greater percentage of Executive Directors at Wealth Creators are satisfied with their total compensation package than their counterparts at Wealth Preservers (Exhibit 7.6), which is usually a result of the performance-based compensation models mentioned above. They're also more likely to be satisfied with their responsibilities at the family office due to the close alignment between the family office's wealth management orientation and their personal financial goals.

EXHIBIT 7.6:

## Satisfaction by Orientation

N = 903 Family Offices

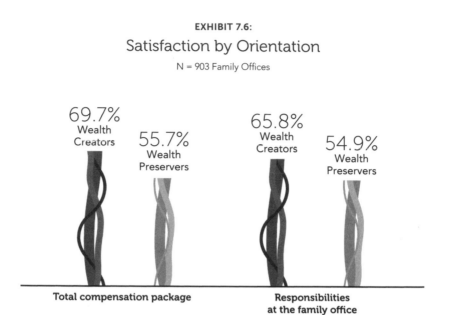

**69.7%**
Wealth
Creators

**55.7%**
Wealth
Preservers

**65.8%**
Wealth
Creators

**54.9%**
Wealth
Preservers

**Total compensation package**

**Responsibilities
at the family office**

In total, about 60% of Executive Directors say there is a strong correlation between their remuneration and specific performance goals of the family office (Exhibit 7.7). Just one-quarter feel they are not being appropriately rewarded for their contribution and less than 5% expect payment structures to meaningfully change over the near term.

EXHIBIT 7.7:

## Perspectives on Compensation

N = 903 Family Offices

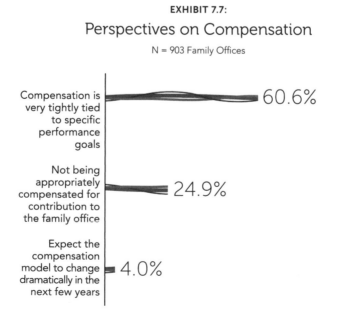

Compensation is
very tightly tied
to specific
performance
goals
**60.6%**

Not being
appropriately
compensated for
contribution to
the family office
**24.9%**

Expect the
compensation
model to change
dramatically in the
next few years
**4.0%**

When segmented by office type, it's clear that MFOs do a better job linking the compensation of Executive Directors to the goals of the business, which translate into higher satisfaction with current pay levels (Exhibit 7.8). By contrast, less than half of Executive Directors at SFOs see a tight link between their earnings and the family office's objectives and slightly more feel undervalued and underpaid for their part in the organization's success.

**EXHIBIT 7.8:**

# Perspectives on Compensation by Type

N = 903 Family Offices

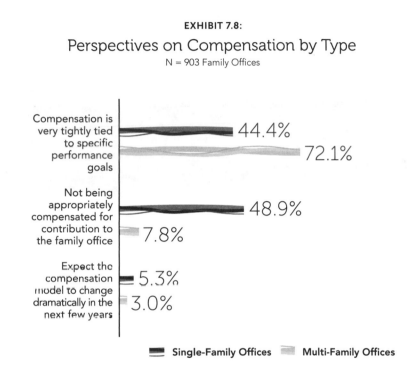

The top professionals at firms with a wealth creation orientation see a closer correlation between their compensation than their counterparts at wealth preservation firms and, as such, leaders at Wealth Creators are more likely to feel that their annual pay is appropriate (Exhibit 7.9).

**EXHIBIT 7.9:**

# Perspectives on Compensation by Orientation

N = 903 Family Offices

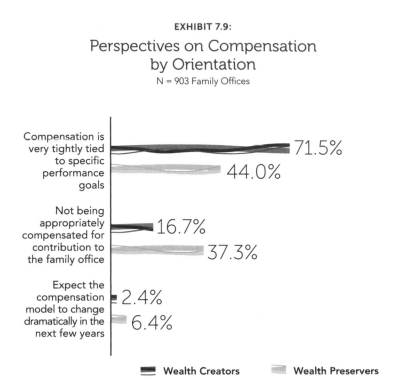

In the next chapter we examine the business and interpersonal skills, the technical competency and the experience needed to function effectively as an Executive Director.

# What It Takes

As with any specialist, being an Executive Director at a family office calls for a specific suite of skills that allows the organization to run like a well-oiled machine. This chapter looks at three specific areas—business and interpersonal skills, technical expertise, and general experience—and the way most Executive Directors found their current positions.

## BUSINESS AND INTERPERSONAL SKILLS

More than nine out of ten Executive Directors cited leadership and management skills as critical, followed closely by the ability to run a business well (Exhibit 8.1). This shows that, with or without the involvement of the family, these entities are perceived as businesses. The Executive Director must be able to run the family office as a functional and effective operating company while also managing the array of interpersonal relationships that allow the business to operate smoothly. These relationships run the gamut from the family members to staff, vendors and suppliers. About 80% cite the importance of communication skills and about three-quarters identify negotiation skills as a must-have. Lowest on the list, at just 44%, were marketing and sales skills.

EXHIBIT 8.1:

# Business and Interpersonal Skills Rated "Very" or "Extremely" Important

N = 903 Family Offices

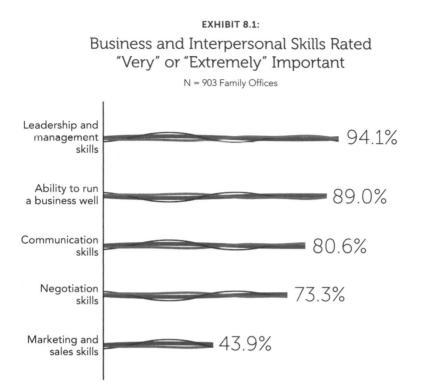

| | |
|---|---|
| Leadership and management skills | 94.1% |
| Ability to run a business well | 89.0% |
| Communication skills | 80.6% |
| Negotiation skills | 73.3% |
| Marketing and sales skills | 43.9% |

When comparing the perspectives of SFOs and MFOs, we find the greatest difference relative to the sales and marketing skills of the Executive Director (Exhibit 8.2). In multi-family offices, nearly 75% of the Executive Directors said this was a critical skill set as compared to just 3% of the single-family offices. It's not surprising that in SFOs the Executive Directors are not interested in sales and marketing as these family offices are typically not planning to solicit new business or heighten their profile. In contrast, MFOs expect the Executive Director to source and close new business with the financial elite.

**EXHIBIT 8.2:**

# Business and Interpersonal Skills Rated "Very" or "Extremely" Important by Type

N = 903 Family Offices

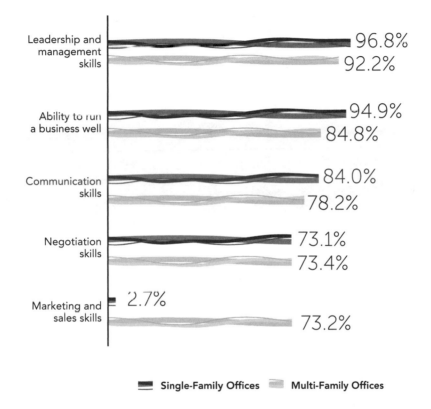

**■ Single-Family Offices    ■ Multi-Family Offices**

While there are incremental differences with respect to the importance of various interpersonal and business skills between Wealth Creators and Wealth Preservers, there's no set of skills that strongly differentiates the two (Exhibit 8.3).

**EXHIBIT 8.3:**

# Business and Interpersonal Skills Rated "Very" or "Extremely" Important by Orientation

N = 903 Family Offices

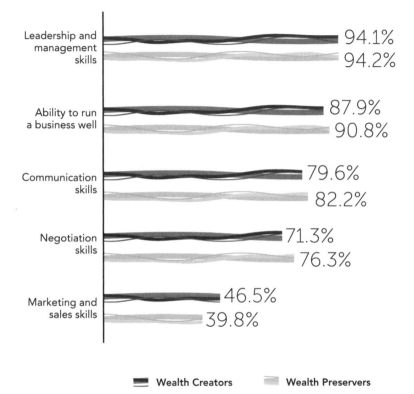

| | | |
|---|---|---|
| Leadership and management skills | | 94.1% |
| | | 94.2% |
| Ability to run a business well | | 87.9% |
| | | 90.8% |
| Communication skills | | 79.6% |
| | | 82.2% |
| Negotiation skills | | 71.3% |
| | | 76.3% |
| Marketing and sales skills | | 46.5% |
| | | 39.8% |

▬▬ Wealth Creators     ▬▬ Wealth Preservers

# TECHNICAL EXPERTISE

Our research shows that Executive Directors feel technical expertise is less critical than business and interpersonal skills, due to the scope of their roles and the ability to work with third-party experts and specialists (Exhibit 8.4). The area most commonly cited by Executive Directors was investment expertise, which is often the background and specialization of many top family office executives.

**EXHIBIT 8.4:**

## Importance of Technical Expertise

N = 903 Family Offices

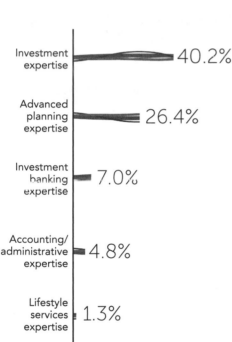

| | |
|---|---|
| Investment expertise | 40.2% |
| Advanced planning expertise | 26.4% |
| Investment banking expertise | 7.0% |
| Accounting/ administrative expertise | 4.8% |
| Lifestyle services expertise | 1.3% |

For the most part, the type and orientation of the family office did not meaningfully influence the way the Executive Directors felt about the importance of technical expertise however those professionals at MFOs were most likely to emphasize investment capabilities (Exhibits 8.5). While Wealth Creators and Wealth Preservers were split between investment know-how and advanced planning knowledge, respectively (Exhibit 8.6).

**EXHIBIT 8.5:**

# Importance of Technical Expertise by Type

N = 903 Family Offices

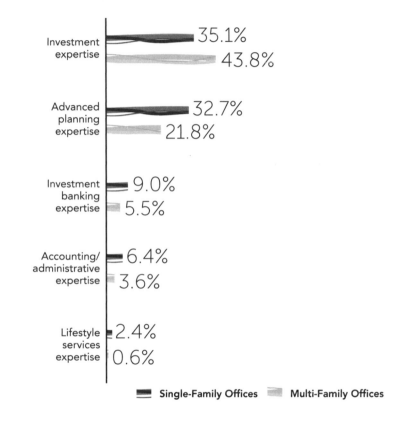

Investment expertise — 35.1% / 43.8%

Advanced planning expertise — 32.7% / 21.8%

Investment banking expertise — 9.0% / 5.5%

Accounting/administrative expertise — 6.4% / 3.6%

Lifestyle services expertise — 2.4% / 0.6%

■ **Single-Family Offices**　■ **Multi-Family Offices**

**EXHIBIT 8.6:**

# Importance of Technical Expertise by Orientation
### N = 903 Family Offices

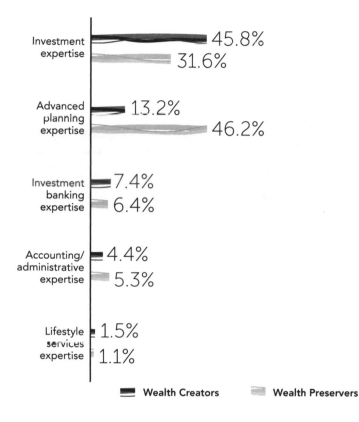

# EXPERIENCE

The large majority of Executive Directors felt that it was more important to have experience interacting with wealthy individuals and families than it was working in a family office environment (Exhibit 8.7)

**EXHIBIT 8.7:**

## Importance of Previous Experience

N = 903 Family Offices

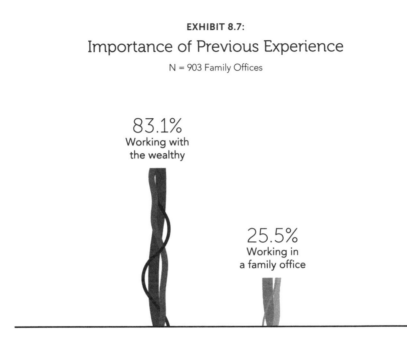

83.1%
Working with
the wealthy

25.5%
Working in
a family office

We get some additional insight on this viewpoint when the research findings are segmented by office type. Both SFOs and MFOs rank experience with the high-net-worth above experience at a family office, but half of Executive Directors at SFOs underscored the importance of familiarity with the family office environment as compared to less than 10% of those professionals at MFOs (Exhibit 8.8).

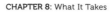

EXHIBIT 8.8:

# Importance of Previous Experience by Type

N = 903 Family Offices

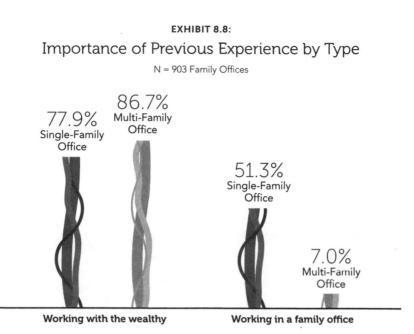

77.9%
Single-Family
Office

86.7%
Multi-Family
Office

51.3%
Single-Family
Office

7.0%
Multi-Family
Office

**Working with the wealthy**          **Working in a family office**

Proportionately speaking, executives at Wealth Creators and Wealth Preservers feel the same about experience levels, although firms with a wealth preservation orientation were more likely to rate the skill as essential to the ongoing operation of the family office (Exhibit 8.9)

**EXHIBIT 8.9:**

# Importance of Previous Experience by Orientation
N = 903 Family Offices

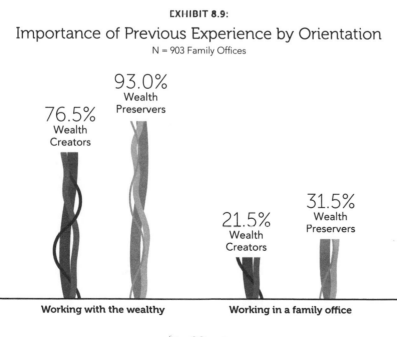

93.0%
Wealth
Preservers

76.5%
Wealth
Creators

21.5%
Wealth
Creators

31.5%
Wealth
Preservers

**Working with the wealthy**          **Working in a family office**

# BECOMING A FAMILY OFFICE
## EXECUTIVE DIRECTOR

The route to any employment opportunity can be varied, but most Executive Directors attribute their current positions to some form of professional networking. More than 40% say their role came about through professional contacts and about one-quarter link it to a previous professional relationship (Exhibit 8.10). Far fewer, just 18%, say they found their current jobs through personal contacts and less than 10% worked with a recruiting firm or survived an intra-firm transition.

EXHIBIT 8.10:

## How the Executive Directors Got Their Jobs

N = 903 Family Offices

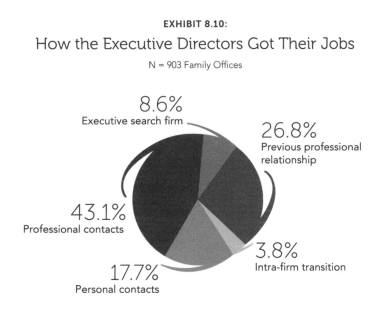

**8.6%**
Executive search firm

**26.8%**
Previous professional relationship

**43.1%**
Professional contacts

**3.8%**
Intra-firm transition

**17.7%**
Personal contacts

Professional contacts and relationships play a much greater role at SFOs than at MFOs (Exhibit 8.11). This is not surprising, since most ultra-wealthy individuals rely on some form of referrals when seeking a new service or professional relationship. At the same time, MFOs are more likely to use a search firm when attempting to locate qualified candidates to run the organization which is consistent with most business-oriented environments.

EXHIBIT 8.11:

# How the Executive Directors Got Their Jobs by Type

N = 903 Family Offices

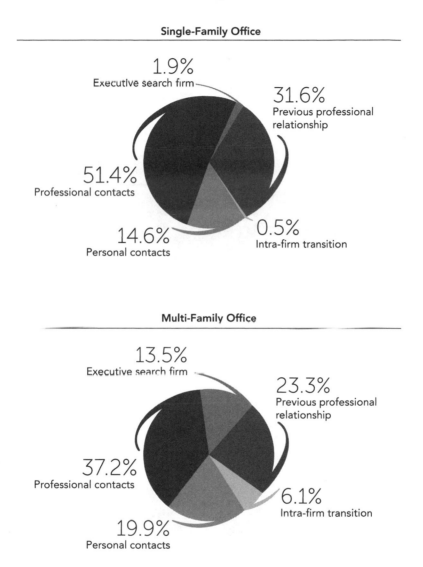

**Single-Family Office**

1.9%
Executive search firm

31.6%
Previous professional relationship

51.4%
Professional contacts

14.6%
Personal contacts

0.5%
Intra-firm transition

**Multi-Family Office**

13.5%
Executive search firm

23.3%
Previous professional relationship

37.2%
Professional contacts

6.1%
Intra-firm transition

19.9%
Personal contacts

Wealth Creators and Wealth Preservers have more consistent views on the subject, valuing professional contacts and relationships above all else (Exhibit 8.12).

EXHIBIT 8.12:

## How the Executive Directors Got Their Jobs by Orientation

N = 903 Family Offices

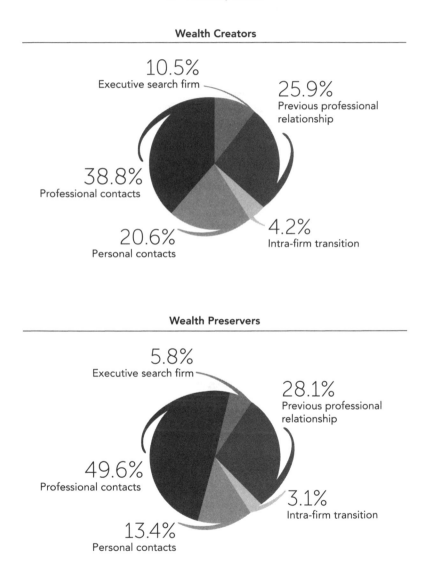

**Wealth Creators**

10.5%
Executive search firm

25.9%
Previous professional relationship

38.8%
Professional contacts

4.2%
Intra-firm transition

20.6%
Personal contacts

**Wealth Preservers**

5.8%
Executive search firm

28.1%
Previous professional relationship

49.6%
Professional contacts

3.1%
Intra-firm transition

13.4%
Personal contacts

The next two sections discuss in detail the range of wealth management and support services offered at today's family offices.

# The Empire Builder

# The Empire Builder

By Russ Alan Prince and Hannah Shaw Grove

*A pig carcass hangs from a chain attached to the ceiling. It weighs about 200 pounds. The appeal of pig flesh is its similarity to human flesh. With three or four passes of her specially made tessen, the pig carcass is sliced in two—half now lies on the floor. Her mastery with the tessen, her expertise at silat, her standing as an Adept at the Play of 7 Knives, her ability to exhaust a quintet of architecturally large concubines, are all indicative of her determination and drive. However, nothing compels her more then amassing Croesus-like levels of wealth.*

Her empire was built over decades. She has become exceptionally wealthy many times over. We don't really know the dividing line between her money and the enterprises she controls. Many times they're one and the same. Nevertheless, there's no question that she's phenomenally rich. In accord with the Money Rules, it's evident that she's highly centered. In this respect, she's a laser beam anthropomorphized. Moreover, having watched her evolution—although she's a natural—she learned to masterfully exploit her extraordinary capabilities. She excelled because of the lessons learned well from her errors in judgment.

## *Learning to Lead*

She has a few—very few—extraordinary abilities. Beyond her steel will, she has a genius for leveraging the talents and skills of others. Not many people are able to optimize and capitalize on their own exceptional capabilities. She is able to show them how this can be accomplished and how they will greatly benefit.

The conundrum is that not everyone she's interested in leveraging is positively inclined to follow her. Aside from knowing how their various abilities can be fit into her business enterprises in a way that solidly benefits her personal immediate objectives which, in turn, build her vast fortune, she has to motivate them which leads to her other extraordinary ability.

It's her talent to very quickly size people up and intuitively recognizing what motivates them. While, we would argue this is an instinctual talent, it has been refined, if not perfected, in the crucible of failure. There have been a plethora of times that she has misjudged people. But, it's more than that for she has many times misjudged her own capacity to help them be more expansive in their thinking and actions. This led to more than a few particularly costly mistakes. However, each failure was a step to great success. Each failure was converted into an opportunity to become more proficient.

For her, every failure was another occasion to learn how to be more effective the next time. And there's always a next time. To become more competent, she would carefully dissect every lost situation, every talent that chose to go a different path. Acknowledging that her failures were all of her own making, she would carefully identify where she miscalculated, where ego overrode reality and she projected her intent onto others, where she simply misread the needs and wants of people. They were often difficult experiences to relive with clarity and objectivity. Doing so, however, always proved fruitful.

Because she embraced her failures and learned from them, she was able to develop a more sophisticated understanding of the motivations of others and how to better incentivize them. Over the years her success rate exponentially improved. From the very beginning, for inspiration, she always turns to a quote from La Rochefoucauld who said, "If we resist our passions, it's more from their weakness than from our strengths."

She fruitfully committed her life to amassing extreme wealth. From the beginning, she devoted herself to becoming a billionaire and was willing to do whatever it took to reach that financial apex. Even today, she's driven to garner ever-greater wealth and is still incredibly willing to do whatever it takes—not being tempered by age or the sizeable fortune already created or the difficulties of ongoing leadership. Wealth accumulation is her obsession and it's become easier because she has learned brilliance from her errors.

## How Far Does a Person Need to Go?

For many of the super-rich, wealth is like seawater—the more you drink the thirstier you get. As we've noted, extreme wealth creation, for many, borders on obsession—as in this situation. To keep drinking, many of the super-rich have to push the envelope, but that isn't a requirement. The wealthy can follow the Money Rules and never have to cross over from the white into the gray—and, they should never go into the black.

The experiences of ethnologically studying as well as consulting with a select number of the super-rich—the Children of Midas—are quite varied, periodically ironic and always entertaining in some of the most unexpected ways. Over time—sometimes lubricated by alcohol—they've shared some of their more intimate and informative stories. These "glimpses behind the curtain" have been the most illuminating and educational. What we see is not the sanitized version of exceptional economic success. Instead, we're in the trenches where personalities dominate, where deals are made and wealth flows.

The ability for a person to radically boost his or her net worth by understanding and using the Money Rules as a guide is not particularly difficult. The mindset and behaviors are not secrets—far from it. In the end, it's all about actualization. In creating Personal Wealth Creation Programs for our few select wealthy clients, we cannot emphasize enough that their commitment is unquestionably the most important factor in their realization of extreme wealth and that certainly includes the often painful process of critically evaluating their mistakes.

PART IV

# Wealth Management

# Investment Management

Family offices are, by definition, coordinating organizations for a family's personal and financial affairs. As such, the vast majority of family offices are organized around an investment function as a way to take an active role in how the family's wealth is managed. Roughly 80% of single-family offices manage money (Exhibit 9.1) and offices that are oriented toward wealth creation are even more likely to do so as investing is a critical part of growing and enhancing a personal fortune (Exhibit 9.2).

**EXHIBIT 9.1:**

## Manage Money in the Single-Family Office
N = 376 Single-Family Offices

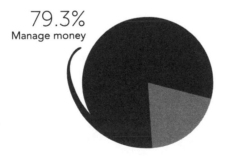

79.3%
Manage money

EXHIBIT 9.2:

**EXHIBIT 9.2:**

# Manage Money in the Single-Family Office by Orientation

N = 298 Single-Family Offices

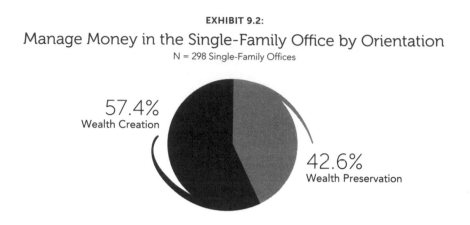

57.4%
Wealth Creation

42.6%
Wealth Preservation

## INSIDE AND OUT

Like many capabilities, investing can be done in-house or through outside agents. The following section discusses responses from all 527 of the multi-family offices in our study and the 79.3% of single-family offices, identified in Exhibit 9.1, about their investment functions. Nearly all of the family offices in our survey select and monitor the efforts of third-party asset managers, while just 38% have an internal, staffed investment capability (Exhibit 9.3).

**EXHIBIT 9.3:**

## Inside and Out

N = 825 Family Offices

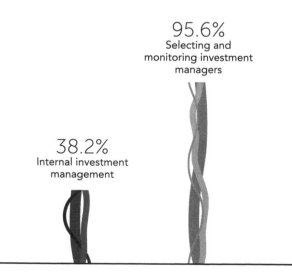

95.6%
Selecting and
monitoring investment
managers

38.2%
Internal investment
management

Multi-family offices are more likely than single-family offices to invest using both approaches (Exhibit 9.4).

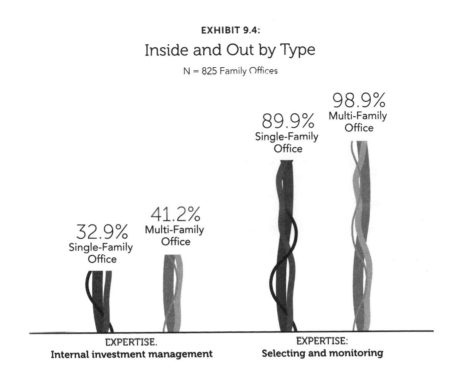

**EXHIBIT 9.4:**

# Inside and Out by Type

N = 825 Family Offices

98.9%
Multi-Family
Office

89.9%
Single-Family
Office

41.2%
Multi-Family
Office

32.9%
Single-Family
Office

EXPERTISE.
**Internal investment management**

EXPERTISE:
**Selecting and monitoring**

The way an office invests is, however, influenced by the objectives of the underlying families. Family offices that are oriented toward wealth creation are far more likely to have an internal capability than those that are oriented toward wealth preservation. By contrast, virtually all Wealth Preservers offices work with outside investment experts as compared to just one-third of Wealth Creators (Exhibit 9.5).

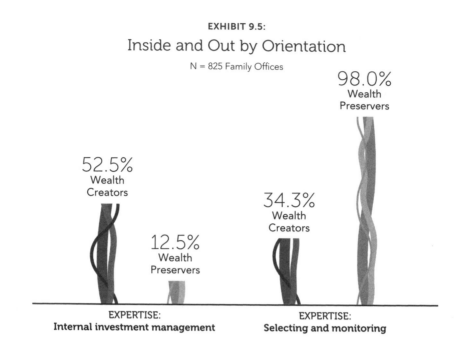

EXHIBIT 9.5:

# Inside and Out by Orientation

N = 825 Family Offices

**98.0%**
Wealth
Preservers

**52.5%**
Wealth
Creators

**34.3%**
Wealth
Creators

**12.5%**
Wealth
Preservers

EXPERTISE:
**Internal investment management**

EXPERTISE:
**Selecting and monitoring**

## ATTENTIVE TO PERSONAL TAX ISSUES

When it comes to the wealthy, taxes play an extremely big part of their financial lives. For instance, the tax efficiency of a portfolio is impacted by the trading philosophy, the ability to harvest losses, and the like.

About half the family offices engaged in investment management are "very" or "extremely" attentive to personal tax issues (Exhibit 9.6). There's no difference between single- and multi-family offices (Exhibit 9.7), however, nearly all the Wealth Preservers are laser focused on personal tax issues while only about a quarter of the Wealth Creators are so focused (Exhibit 9.8).

EXHIBIT 9.6:

# "Very" or "Extremely" Attentive to Personal Tax Issues

N = 825 Family Offices

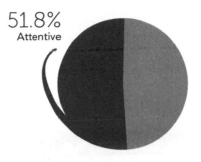

51.8%
Attentive

EXHIBIT 9.7:

# "Very" or "Extremely" Attentive to Personal Tax Issues by Type

N = 825 Family Offices

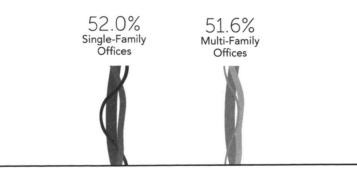

52.0%
Single-Family
Offices

51.6%
Multi-Family
Offices

**EXHIBIT 9.8:**

# "Very" or "Extremely" Attentive to Personal Tax Issues by Orientation

N = 825 Family Offices

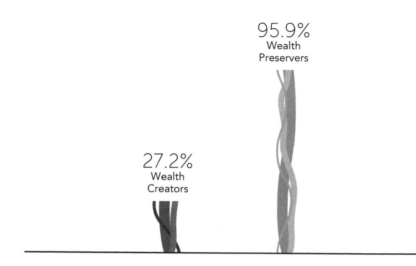

95.9%
Wealth
Preservers

27.2%
Wealth
Creators

For Wealth Preservers the goal is all about enabling the financial elite to maintain their fortunes. They are more likely to employ wealth enhancement strategies (see *Chapter 10: Advanced Planning Services*). For example, they might employ multiple jurisdictions and leverage the tax treaties to lessen the tax bite on the growth in their investment portfolio. In contrast, Wealth Creators tend to look for absolute returns.

## ALTERNATIVE INVESTMENTS

Alternative investments cover a large range of possibilities. Nearly 70% of the family offices are investing in alternatives (Exhibit 9.9). Three-quarters of the multi-family offices and about 60% of the single-family offices make alternatives a part of their investment portfolios (Exhibit 9.10). Alternative investments are generally a means for building wealth. As such about 85% of Wealth Creators are using them (Exhibit 9.11). Meanwhile, only 38% of Wealth Preservers are incorporating them into their portfolios.

**EXHIBIT 9.9:**

# Alternative Investing
N = 825 Family Offices

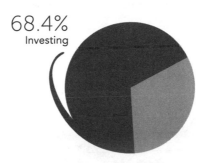

68.4%
Investing

---

**EXHIBIT 9.10:**

## Alternative Investing by Type

N = 825 Family Offices

**EXHIBIT 9.11**

## Alternative Investing by Orientation

N = 825 Family Offices

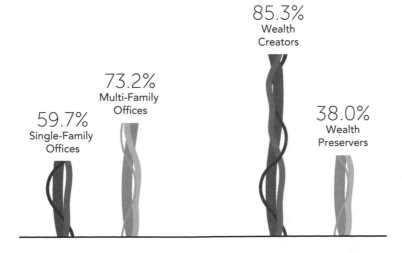

59.7%
Single-Family
Offices

73.2%
Multi-Family
Offices

85.3%
Wealth
Creators

38.0%
Wealth
Preservers

# HEDGE FUNDS

Within the category of alternative investments, hedge funds have the upper hand when it comes to popularity and use. Nearly all family offices that invest in alternatives use hedge funds as part of their portfolios (Exhibit 9.12), and there is no meaningful difference when the responses are segmented by office type or orientation (Exhibits 9.13 and 9.14).

**EXHIBIT 9.12:**

## Investing in Hedge Funds
N = 564 Family Offices

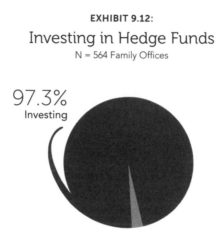

97.3%
Investing

**EXHIBIT 9.13:**

## Investing in Hedge Funds by Type
N = 564 Family Offices

**EXHIBIT 9.14:**

## Investing in Hedge Funds by Orientation
N = 564 Family Offices

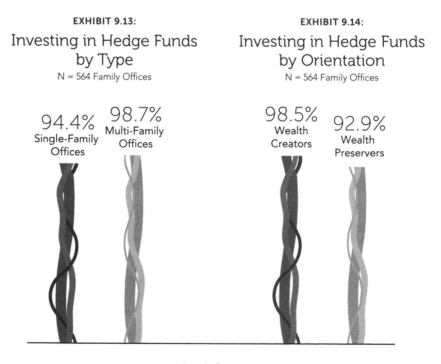

94.4%
Single-Family Offices

98.7%
Multi-Family Offices

98.5%
Wealth Creators

92.9%
Wealth Preservers

# PRIVATE EQUITY

About two-thirds of the family offices that invest in alternatives choose to engage in private equity transactions (Exhibit 9.15). When segmented by office type, we find that 71% of multi-family offices and 57% of single-family offices have private equity investments (Exhibit 9.16), and there is virtually no difference in usage level between Wealth Creators and Wealth Preservers (Exhibit 9.17).

**EXHIBIT 9.15:**

## Investing in Private Equity
N = 564 Family Offices

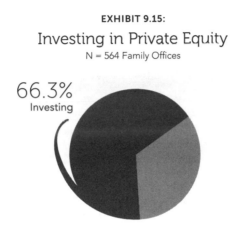

66.3%
Investing

| **EXHIBIT 9.16:** | **EXHIBIT 9.17:** |
|---|---|
| Investing in Private Equity by Type | Investing in Private Equity by Orientation |
| N = 564 Family Offices | N = 564 Family Offices |

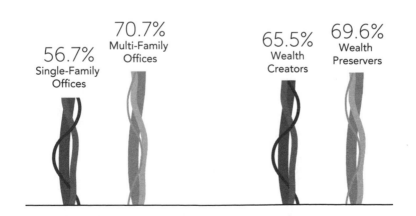

56.7%
Single-Family
Offices

70.7%
Multi-Family
Offices

65.5%
Wealth
Creators

69.6%
Wealth
Preservers

# PRIVATE EQUITY INVESTMENT ALIGNMENT

Of the family offices investing in private equity, we found that more than one quarter of them are seeking a high level of alignment with the way they created their wealth (Exhibit 9.18). This means that they're inclined to invest in funds and business ventures that are similar to the way they created their fortunes. So, if a family made its money in banking and they have a high level of alignment, the family is predisposed to invest in banks or funds that invest in banks.

**EXHIBIT 9.18:**

## High Levels of Alignment with Source of Wealth

N = 374 Family Offices

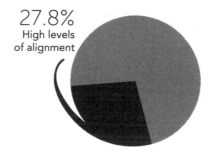

27.8%
High levels
of alignment

Proportionately more single-family offices investing in private equity are highly aligned compared to multi-family offices (Exhibit 9.19). This has a lot to do with the fact that MFOs unless they're directed by a particular family or families, are more likely to be agnostic in this regard. Meanwhile, a greater percentage of Wealth Preservers compared to Wealth Creators are likely to seek alignment (Exhibit 9.20). Here, the Wealth Preservers have a higher comfort level with what made them wealthy and feel better able to understand the investment and calculate the risks involved.

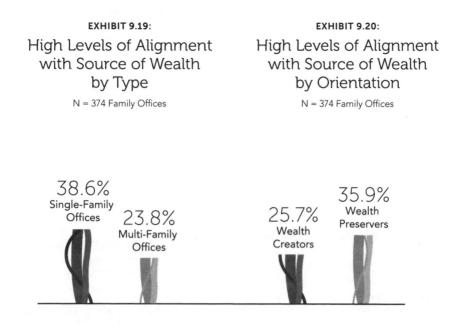

**EXHIBIT 9.19:**

## High Levels of Alignment with Source of Wealth by Type

N = 374 Family Offices

**EXHIBIT 9.20:**

## High Levels of Alignment with Source of Wealth by Orientation

N = 374 Family Offices

38.6%
Single-Family
Offices

23.8%
Multi-Family
Offices

25.7%
Wealth
Creators

35.9%
Wealth
Preservers

What proves instructive is that these family offices interested in aligned investment opportunities are very interested in committing substantial monies to private equity deals or funds they believe themselves to understand quite well. They're much more interested in this approach than in a diversified investment portfolio. However, the anecdotal evidence indicates that private equity firms are more interested in pushing their wares than identifying family offices that are interested and good fits for their products.

# Advanced Planning Services

B eing able to help a family with its full span of financial needs often means the ability to deliver advanced planning services, or those areas of specialization that relate to estate planning, tax mitigation and wealth enhancement as well as asset protection planning. About two-thirds of family offices in our survey say they provide or coordinate wealth transfer services to their clientele, whereas just 10% deliver wealth enhancement expertise and even fewer, just 7% offer asset protection. (Exhibit 10.1).

**EXHIBIT 10.1:**

## Provide or Coordinate Advanced Planning Services

N = 903 Family Offices

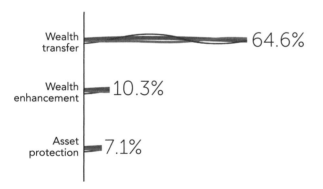

Uses of these services vary, however, when viewed by office type and orientation. About three-quarters of multi-family offices help their clients with wealth transfer and estate planning efforts versus just half of single-family offices. SFOs were slightly more likely to provide wealth enhancement and asset protection services than MFOs (Exhibit 10.2)

**EXHIBIT 10.2:**

## Provide or Coordinate Advanced Planning Services by Type

N = 903 Family Offices

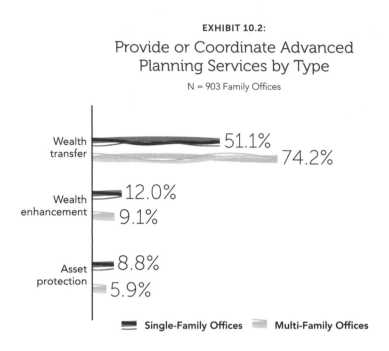

**EXHIBIT 10.3** Single-Family Offices    Multi-Family Offices

Across the board, Wealth Preservers were more likely to include a selection of advanced planning capabilities as part of their platform than any of the Wealth Creators (Exhibit 10.3).

**EXHIBIT 10.3:**

## Provide or Coordinate Advanced Planning Services by Orientation

N = 903 Family Offices

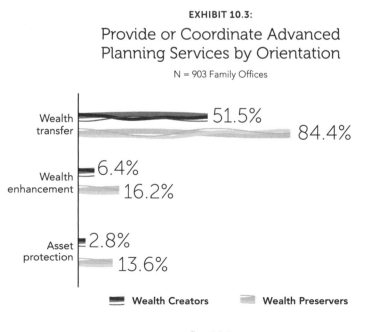

Wealth Creators    Wealth Preservers

# RELIANCE ON OUTSIDE COUNSEL

Due to the highly specialized nature of advanced planning, nearly all of the 649 family offices that are providing or coordinating such services rely heavily on outside legal counsel to do so (Exhibit 10.4).

**EXHIBIT 10.4:**

## Reliance on Outside Counsel

N = 649 Family Offices

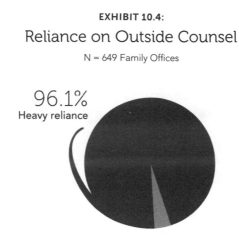

96.1%
Heavy reliance

Most family offices choose to work with third-party legal professionals rather than having such experts on staff because the need is intermittent and it's a way to manage fixed costs (Exhibit 10.5). About two-thirds of family offices say that turning to outside specialists allows them to source the best possible professional for each case and allows them to avoid the responsibility of continuing education and staying abreast of trends and regulatory changes.

**EXHIBIT 10.5:**

## Rationale

N = 624 Family Offices

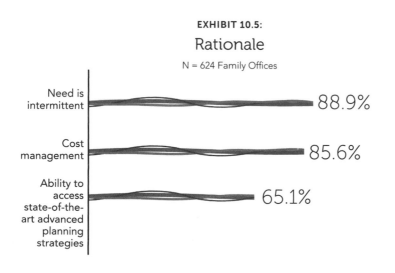

Need is intermittent — 88.9%

Cost management — 85.6%

Ability to access state-of-the-art advanced planning strategies — 65.1%

When segmented by office type, we see that multi-family offices are motivated more by the ability to curtail costs while single-family offices prefer the flexibility that working with contractors allows them when it comes to selecting the best expert for the situation (Exhibit 10.6).

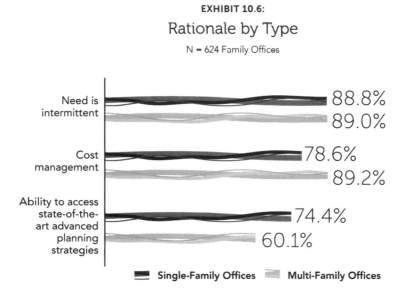

## Rationale by Type

N = 624 Family Offices

| | Single-Family Offices | Multi-Family Offices |
|---|---|---|
| Need is intermittent | 88.8% | 89.0% |
| Cost management | 78.6% | 89.2% |
| Ability to access state-of-the-art advanced planning strategies | 74.4% | 60.1% |

Single-Family Offices    Multi-Family Offices

Many advanced planning techniques are core to the premise of wealth preservation, so it's not surprising to find that the offices with that kind of orientation were well versed in how to achieve the greatest results in the most efficient manner (Exhibit 10.7).

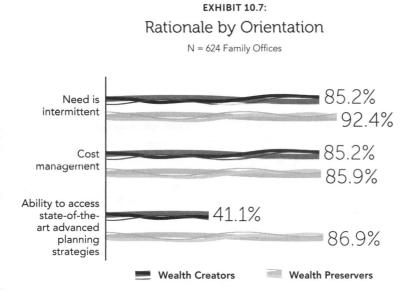

**EXHIBIT 10.7:**

# Rationale by Orientation

N = 624 Family Offices

| | Wealth Creators | Wealth Preservers |
|---|---|---|
| Need is intermittent | 85.2% | 92.4% |
| Cost management | 85.2% | 85.9% |
| Ability to access state-of-the-art advanced planning strategies | 41.1% | 86.9% |

■ **Wealth Creators**    ■ **Wealth Preservers**

# Private Investment Banking

oday very few family offices, regardless of type or orientation, are providing private investment banking services to their underlying families (Exhibit 11.1). It's worth noting, however, that single-family offices and Wealth Creators are more likely to do so than their counterparts (Exhibits 11.2 and 11.3). We expect interest in this type of service to increase in coming years as family offices cement their reputation as the 'go to' resource for the ultra-affluent.

**EXHIBIT 11.1:**

## Provide or Coordinate Private Investment Banking Services

N = 903 Family Offices

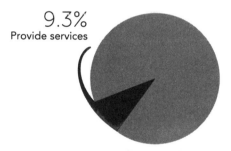

9.3%
Provide services

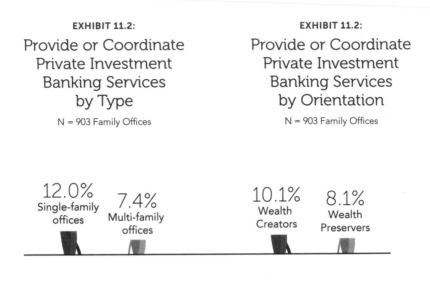

**EXHIBIT 11.2:**

## Provide or Coordinate Private Investment Banking Services by Type

N = 903 Family Offices

**EXHIBIT 11.2:**

## Provide or Coordinate Private Investment Banking Services by Orientation

N = 903 Family Offices

**12.0%**
Single-family offices

**7.4%**
Multi-family offices

**10.1%**
Wealth Creators

**8.1%**
Wealth Preservers

Of the family offices that make private investment banking available to their underlying families, most are focused on making deals rather than financing them (Exhibit 11.4).

**EXHIBIT 11.4:**

## Types of Private Investment Banking Services

N = 84 Family Offices

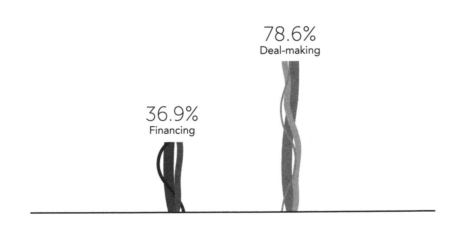

**78.6%**
Deal-making

**36.9%**
Financing

Because family offices are highly customized entities, it stands to reason that financing is used to back a broad range of opportunities that surface through extended family members, friends, business associates and professionals. The most common type of venture was investment-related, though one-third of family offices put money toward corporate and lifestyle enterprises as well (Exhibit 11.5).

**EXHIBIT 11.5:**
## Types of Financing
N = 31 Family Offices

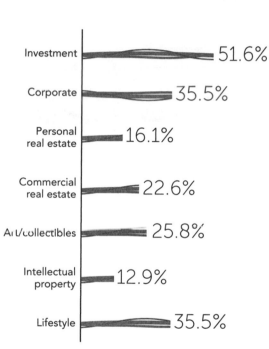

| | |
|---|---|
| Investment | 51.6% |
| Corporate | 35.5% |
| Personal real estate | 16.1% |
| Commercial real estate | 22.6% |
| Art/collectibles | 25.8% |
| Intellectual property | 12.9% |
| Lifestyle | 35.5% |

Actively managing tax burdens on such deals is a secondary consideration for most, as just 10% claimed they were highly attentive to such concerns (Exhibit 11.6).

EXHIBIT 11.6:
# "Very" or "Extremely" Attentive to Personal Tax Issues
N = 31 Family Offices

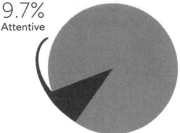

9.7%
Attentive

Almost three-quarters of the deals were categorized as a merger or acquisition, though other areas were also represented at much lower levels (Exhibit 11.7).

EXHIBIT 11.7:
# Types of Deal Making
N = 66 Family Offices

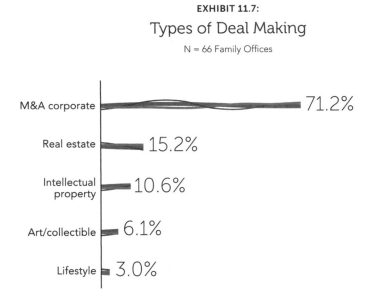

| | |
|---|---|
| M&A corporate | 71.2% |
| Real estate | 15.2% |
| Intellectual property | 10.6% |
| Art/collectible | 6.1% |
| Lifestyle | 3.0% |

There is a slightly higher concern for the tax consequences of a deal when compared to the focus as part of the financing process, but it still remains low relative to the affluent market's professed concerns with the level of taxes and the degree to which they are managed as part of an overall investment objective (Exhibit 11.8).

**EXHIBIT 11.8:**

# "Very" or "Extremely" Attentive to Personal Tax Issues

N = 66 Family Offices

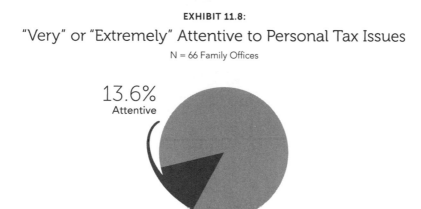

13.6%
Attentive

Most family offices assert that offering investment banking is part of the custom-ized suite of capabilities put in place to meet the needs of underlying families, though a goodly number see the profit potential of such services and find that equally attractive. And while multi-family offices are always searching for ways to separate themselves from competitors, most anticipate other services as a better use of their resources in the current environment (Exhibit 11.9).

**EXHIBIT 11.9:**

## Rationale

N = 84 Family Offices

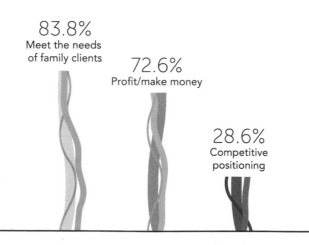

83.8%
Meet the needs
of family clients

72.6%
Profit/make money

28.6%
Competitive
positioning

# *The Gnome*

# The Gnome

By Russ Alan Prince and Hannah Shaw Grove

*He claims to be four feet even. We think he's shorter than four feet, but no one debates the point. He's not a midget or a dwarf. He's just not very tall. It could be that he looks smaller because he's bent over. It's an age thing. We all know that he's close to the end which is why he's pretty forthcoming even if he's obtuse about it. He might be vertically challenged, but inch for inch, he's all blinding intellect and nasty mean.*

*The Gnome—his moniker of choice—is extraordinarily wealthy. He grew up in a family business. As he slowly empties a few wine bottles, he shares how, out of default, he came to first control the family business and then grow it large through carefully orchestrated mergers.*

## A Family in Ruins

He had an older brother who once ran the family business but had to step down because of the "episode." His brother took over the family business when both their parents died in a car accident one rainy night.

As the Gnome tells it, the events forcing his brother out of the family business and what subsequently happened to him was a terrible tragedy. His brother's wife caught him in their bed drunk with the nanny, the family cook and two other women. His brother claims to have no idea about any of this having sworn off liquor and not taken a drop for more than five years. The Gnome and their sister used all their cash to buy out their brother; he desperately needed the money to get through his impending divorce.

The single indiscretion cost his brother his wealth, his family (including access to his three young children), his position in the community and even his health. After the divorce, the brother began drinking heavily ruining any chance of rebuilding his life. He died from a heart attack four years later.

The Gnome also had an older sister. As they were growing up, she always protected him from all the children who bullied and ridiculed him because of his size. She was the one person who had a positive impact on his self-confidence. His sister was never very successful with men. One day she met a truly a captivating man. They were very quickly engaged. Her fiancé understood her and they were amazingly in-synch on everything! The only problem was that he needed a lot of cash to pay off debts. The Gnome came to the rescue. At great expense to himself, he arranged a loan for his sister using all of her shares and some of his shares in the family business as collateral.

With money handed to him, her fiancé disappeared. The Gnome's sister was distraught fearing disaster for her lover. She was also beside herself having lost her shares in the family business as well as a percentage of her devoted younger brother's shares. The Gnome was able to scrape together enough money to keep paying off the loan and eventually took ownership of the shares he and his sister used as collateral. Meanwhile, his sister ended up needing extensive psychiatric care which the Gnome dutifully paid for until her untimely death. These awful circumstances ultimately left the Gnome owning the entire family business.

The Gnome's bad luck didn't end with his family. A big problem he had to repeatedly correct was, as he put it, his poor choice of business partners. The Gnome would sell his company to a larger privately held firm, always for stock. Even though he did an extensive amount of due diligence, before long the senior managers or the families of the merged company would implode.

In one way or another—from being bi-curious and contracting AIDS to experimenting with heroin to being caught taking reprehensible sex tours in Southeast Asia—the bad behavior of the majority owners in the businesses forced the Gnome to come in and become very actively involved. He did this temporarily until professional management could be installed. Concurrently, he bought out the majority owners taking over the firms.

## *Rumor Has It*

The Gnome would always say that he was cursed but resilient. With all the horrendous events, he was always able to soldier through. And, to make matter worse, there are all those mean spirited rumors.

Rumor has it that someone choreographed his brother's tragic episode. It seems that someone may have paid the cook to spike his food and also paid the women to be present when his brother's wife appeared. A year after his wife divorced his brother, she married a much younger man with whom she might or might not have been having an affair.

Rumor has it that the sister's fiancé was a fourth-rate unemployed actor and conman. He knew every button to press, every switch to flip. What's also interesting is that the hard-money lender, like the actor, also disappeared one day. There were also a few other rumors circulating about the fates of the Gnome's business partners. There were four sets of them and rumors have spread concerning their hard luck.

All these events happened a very long time ago. No one really has any documentation as to what precisely occurred. It's just what people remembered and old people's memories can sometimes be quite faulty. Besides, most of the involved parties died long ago.

Today the Gnome is exceedingly wealthy and he wants more, a lot more. It's just that—and it takes us four bottles of his really wonderful wine one long night to get there—he doesn't have the strength to keep amassing wealth. His "system" is just too hard to run at his age. Having known the Gnome for about five years and only getting to really know him well this last year, we see how people think of him as charming and charismatic—exuding love and benevolence. However, we're absolutely certain that he's incapable of compassion or empathy or anything closely resembling kindness.

PART V
# Support Services

# Administrative Services

I ncreasingly, family offices are taking on more of the day-to-day processes that are required to keep a family with significant means operating smoothly. The aggregation of client data is the most prevalent support service available at family offices today and is offered by 60% of them. Less than half of firms surveyed provided assistance with tax returns, bill paying and bookkeeping (Exhibit 12.1).

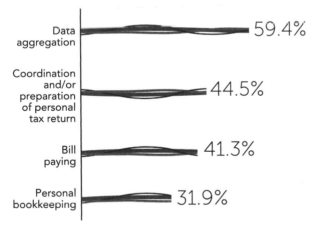

EXHIBIT 12.1:

## Providing or Overseeing Administrative Services

N = 903 Family Offices

| | |
|---|---|
| Data aggregation | 59.4% |
| Coordination and/or preparation of personal tax return | 44.5% |
| Bill paying | 41.3% |
| Personal bookkeeping | 31.9% |

Multi-family offices were far more likely to offer any of the administrative services than their single-family counterparts (Exhibit 12.2), though there was greater balance in the responses when viewed by firm orientation. In fact, the only area with a marked difference between Wealth Creators and Wealth Preservers was data aggregation, which was offered by two-thirds of the former and just half of the latter (Exhibit 12.3).

**EXHIBIT 12.2:**

## Providing or Overseeing Administrative Services by Type

N = 903 Family Offices

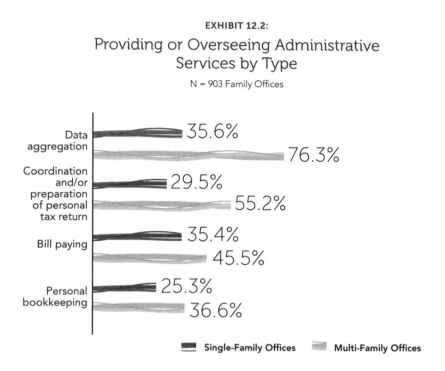

Single-Family Offices    Multi-Family Offices

**EXHIBIT 12.3:**

## Providing or Overseeing Administrative Services by Orientation

N = 903 Family Offices

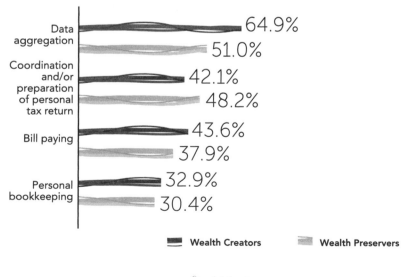

Wealth Creators    Wealth Preservers

Nearly all family offices with such offerings say they help heighten the overall level of service they can deliver to the underlying families, though about half say the range of administrative support they offer is an intrinsic part of the broader platform of offerings and 40% say they are motivated to do so by the profit margins these kinds of services can bring to the business (Exhibit 12.4).

EXHIBIT 12.4:

## Rationale

N = 662 Family Offices

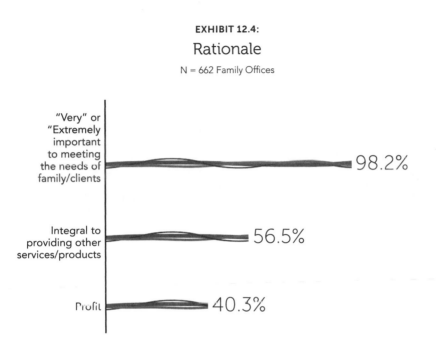

"Very" or "Extremely important to meeting the needs of family/clients — 98.2%

Integral to providing other services/products — 56.5%

Profit — 40.3%

When the responses are segmented by office type, the chance to do a better job for clients remains the top priority for both single- and multi-family offices. Two-thirds of single-family offices cite the relationship between certain administrative services and other offerings as an important consideration, while just one-fifth are motivated by profit. Half of all multi-family offices surveyed say the intrinsic qualities of certain administrative services and their profit are equally persuasive reasons to include them on their platform of offerings (Exhibit 12.5).

EXHIBIT 12.5:
## Rationale by Type
N = 662 Family Offices

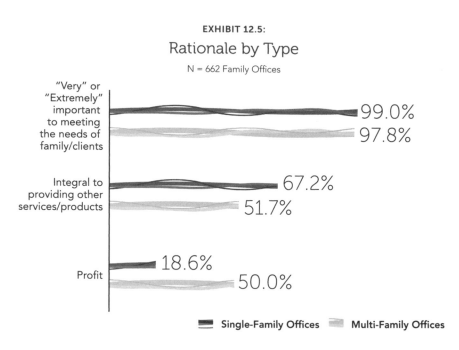

"Very" or "Extremely" important to meeting the needs of family/clients — 99.0% / 97.8%

Integral to providing other services/products — 67.2% / 51.7%

Profit — 18.6% / 50.0%

■ Single-Family Offices   ■ Multi-Family Offices

When viewed by the orientation of the firm, Wealth Preservers are more likely to value the integrated nature and the profit potential of certain administrative services than Wealth Creators are (Exhibit 12.6).

EXHIBIT 12.6:
## Rationale by Orientation
N = 662 Family Offices

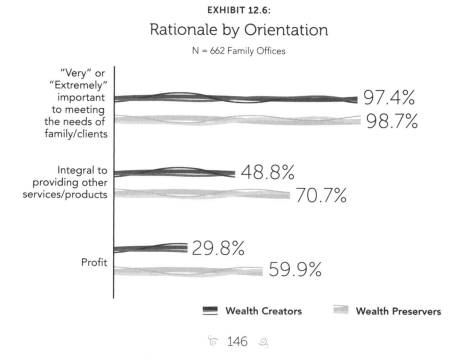

"Very" or "Extremely" important to meeting the needs of family/clients — 97.4% / 98.7%

Integral to providing other services/products — 48.8% / 70.7%

Profit — 29.8% / 59.9%

■ Wealth Creators   ■ Wealth Preservers

It's worth noting that the majority of family offices that engage in these types of services are multi-family offices who see the expansion of their offerings as a competitive distinction (Exhibit 12.7).

# Provides the Multi-Family Office with a Competitive Advantage

N = 458 Multi-Family Offices

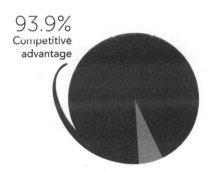

93.9%
Competitive
advantage

# Lifestyle Services

ike administrative services, lifestyle support is not as pervasive among family offices as investment management. Less than half of all firms surveyed offered some type of lifestyle support, with personal security being the most common, followed closely by medical advocacy, concierge services and philanthropic advisory support (Exhibit 13.1). Slightly fewer provided the more specialized services of financial education for family members, assistance developing and managing collections and property management.

**EXHIBIT 13.1:**

## Providing or Overseeing Lifestyle Services

N = 903 Family Offices

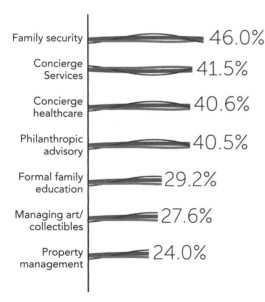

| | |
|---|---|
| Family security | 46.0% |
| Concierge Services | 41.5% |
| Concierge healthcare | 40.6% |
| Philanthropic advisory | 40.5% |
| Formal family education | 29.2% |
| Managing art/collectibles | 27.6% |
| Property management | 24.0% |

Lifestyle offerings are unique and the degree to which they are made available by family offices will depend entirely on the interests and priorities of the underlying families and, as such, may vary over time. The single-family offices in our survey seem to have more experience with a range of lifestyle services, specifically personal security and charitable advisory work, than do multi-family offices (Exhibit 13.2).

**EXHIBIT 13.2:**

## Providing or Overseeing Lifestyle Services by Type

N = 903 Family Offices

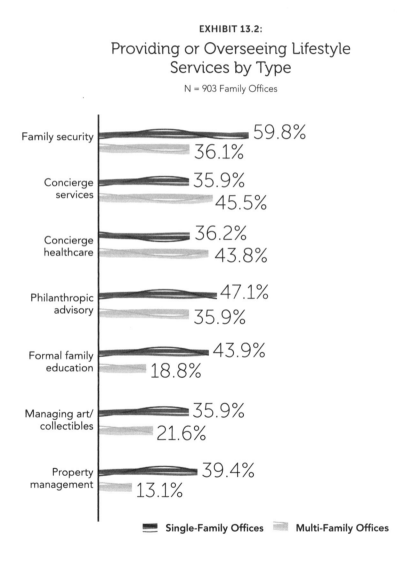

| | Single-Family Offices | Multi-Family Offices |
| --- | --- | --- |
| Family security | 59.8% | 36.1% |
| Concierge services | 35.9% | 45.5% |
| Concierge healthcare | 36.2% | 43.8% |
| Philanthropic advisory | 47.1% | 35.9% |
| Formal family education | 43.9% | 18.8% |
| Managing art/collectibles | 35.9% | 21.6% |
| Property management | 39.4% | 13.1% |

Wealth Preservers, often more risk-averse families, are slightly more likely to offer lifestyle support than Wealth Creators who may be focused on growing their asset base instead of spending it to accomplish specific objectives (Exhibit 13.3).

EXHIBIT 13.3:

## Providing or Overseeing Lifestyle Services by Orientation

N = 903 Family Offices

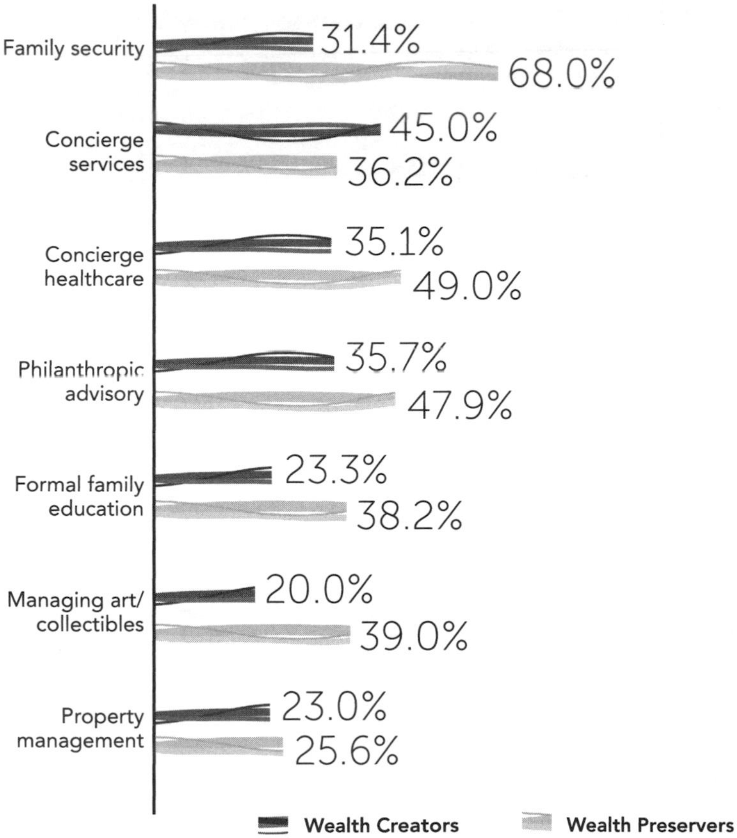

| Category | Wealth Creators | Wealth Preservers |
|---|---|---|
| Family security | 31.4% | 68.0% |
| Concierge services | 45.0% | 36.2% |
| Concierge healthcare | 35.1% | 49.0% |
| Philanthropic advisory | 35.7% | 47.9% |
| Formal family education | 23.3% | 38.2% |
| Managing art/collectibles | 20.0% | 39.0% |
| Property management | 23.0% | 25.6% |

**Wealth Creators**   **Wealth Preservers**

And, as with administrative services, most family offices view their foray into lifestyle support services as a way to deliver a higher-quality of service to underlying families. Given the arbitrary quality of these services, it's not surprising that there is less correlation between them and other offerings on the platform and that it is harder to offer them at consistently high margins (Exhibits 13.4, 13.5 and 13.6).

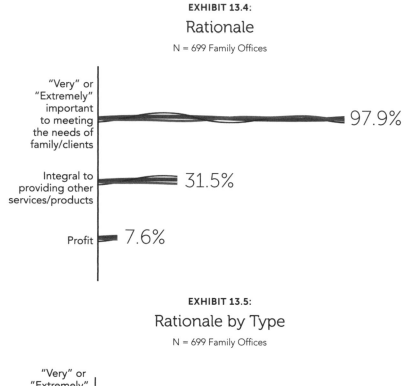

**EXHIBIT 13.4:**
## Rationale
N = 699 Family Offices

- "Very" or "Extremely" important to meeting the needs of family/clients — 97.9%
- Integral to providing other services/products — 31.5%
- Profit — 7.6%

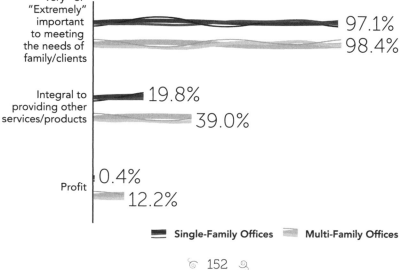

**EXHIBIT 13.5:**
## Rationale by Type
N = 699 Family Offices

- "Very" or "Extremely" important to meeting the needs of family/clients — 97.1% / 98.4%
- Integral to providing other services/products — 19.8% / 39.0%
- Profit — 0.4% / 12.2%

■ **Single-Family Offices** ■ **Multi-Family Offices**

**EXHIBIT 13.6:**

# Rationale by Orientation

N = 699 Family Offices

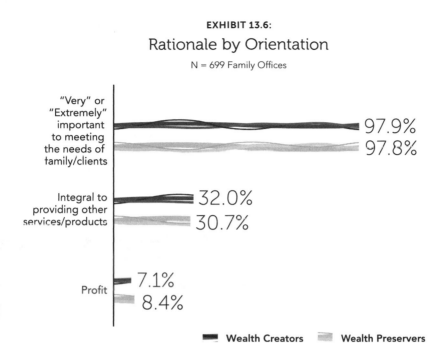

"Very" or "Extremely" important to meeting the needs of family/clients

**97.9%**
**97.8%**

Integral to providing other services/products

**32.0%**
**30.7%**

Profit

**7.1%**
**8.4%**

■■ **Wealth Creators**     ▨ **Wealth Preservers**

Again, multi-family offices perceive such services as a way to distinguish themselves from their competitors (Exhibit 13.7)

**EXHIBIT 13.7:**

# Provides the Multi-Family Office with a Competitive Advantage

N = 426 Multi-Family Offices

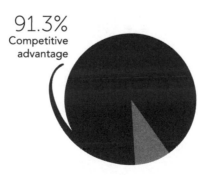

**91.3%**
Competitive advantage

# The Monster Hunter

# The Monster Hunter

By Russ Alan Prince and Hannah Shaw Grove

*Dinner was an over-the-top event with more than a dozen people. As the festivities began to wind down, the three of us retired to an enormous and elaborately furnished suite in a five-star hotel. Though it was one of the largest and most imposing rooms we'd been in, nothing else in the first few moments of our postprandial visit indicated the strange and fascinating experiences to come.*

Our host has always been an enigma; despite moving in the same business circles for at least six years, we knew almost nothing about him. A senior partner at an intentionally small and exceptionally successful private equity firm, he's perfected professional courtesy while remaining coolly distant. In retrospect, he'd been guarded, even noticeably secretive, with personal information. The following hours marked a sea change in our relationship. By morning we'd reached a new level of trust and he allowed us a rare glimpse of the man behind the carefully constructed façade, filling in the sizeable gaps in our understanding of his professional background and its immutable influence on his current role (and successes) at the private equity fund.

Much of what he revealed during our intense and lengthy conversation had never been discussed outside a very exclusive group of law enforcement professionals with the highest levels of security clearance—understandable once we were privy to the terrifying, brutal and oddly fascinating details.

## *There Are Monsters Among Us!*

"I hunted monsters," he explained. "I was great at it and I'm proud of my victories...and I've been devastated by my failures."

He described some of his most difficult cases and how he and his fellow law enforcement professionals ran the monsters to the ground. He told his stories from the heart, including how each case tore at him. How he obsessed and often privately cried over the victims and their families. How, in time, he saw through the eyes of the deranged killers and understood how they ordered their worlds, no matter how convoluted, erratic and disjointed their thinking was.

---

*There was the embezzler who murdered his wife and four young children, as well as both family dogs, because authorities uncovered his financial manipulations and were closing in. He was going to make a run for it and psychologically couldn't justify the hardship his family would face without him. So, applying wonderfully warped logic, killing each and every one of them was the only solution. This way he was ensuring they wouldn't suffer when he vanished. He found the experience of murder so pleasurable that he stayed around, in the shadows, "helping out" other executives by stalking and killing some of their family members. He believed these executives would then be liberated by his largess—no longer encumbered by a loving family whom they also loved.*

*Twin boys were studying philosophy at a university. After deep contemplation, they concluded that some people were selfishly draining the world's resources—a very bad thing. In their minds, these people were stealing from them and other upstanding, concerned citizens. Their answer was to eliminate these "societal parasites." The biggest problem the twins faced was deciding which one of them deserved the right to "do the deed." They solved this problem by flipping a coin for each parasite. They started by slowly poisoning their closest and not-so-closest friends. They knew these people well and concluded that they would never make significant contributions to society. Expanding past their quickly shrinking circle of friends, strangulation became the preferred curative.*

---

*One of his scariest cases, extending over nearly a decade, made Dr. Hannibal Lecter look like a choirboy. What's so horrifying is that this devious, conniving sociopath is real and not a fictional creation. He would meticulously detail the life of a person who "faulted him" by doing something as trivial as cutting him off in traffic or interrupting him at a meeting. He would then stalk them with the intent of eating the offending parts of the victim in front of them before bleeding them out.*

He discussed the cases and how he eventually shifted from being a top-flight criminal profiler to a highly successful private equity investor. As a criminal profiler he never earned very much but he found it fulfilling to lock up psychotically dangerous people. His career was so intense that his wife left him, taking their two young sons with her. He doesn't blame her because of the emotional strain she experienced due to his career.

## The Move Into the "Line of Money"

After more than 20 years hunting monsters, he was badly burned out and had little in his life to show for it. He left his law enforcement position with nothing more than a relatively small civil service pension. "You just don't get rich saving the world," he joked.

After retiring and drinking heavily for about a year, he ran into one of the "financial types" he sometimes crossed paths with during his law enforcement career. The man wanted him to profile the owners of a company his corporate client was interested in acquiring. He declined at first. But, badly in need of money, he soon agreed to the assignment.

"Psychologically dissecting corporate chieftains is straight-up child's play compared to looking into the obsidian blackness that's a criminally vicious sadist," he explained. The investment banker put more faith in his profiling of the business owners than in all the financial analyses his firm concocted. The result was the development and execution of a brilliant negotiation strategy and a transaction that was much more profitable than initially projected. This led to more of the same work.

A couple of years later, he gravitated to private equity, where his "gift for seeing" made him extremely rich. Today, he runs a team of profilers and researchers he recruited from his previous life. He explains that he's not doing anything different from his crime fighting days, but admits it's much easier now that his subjects happily agree to interviews rather than hide in the shadows.

He's a profiler and will always be a profiler. From the perspective of creating a substantial fortune, the only difference is that he's now positioned squarely in the line of money. He employs the same expertise in his current career as he did in his former one. The change is that he's using his skills and talents in a business model that compensates him exceptionally well.

# PART VI

# Emerging Trends

# 14

# Turnarounds & Lift-offs

There's a real desire by many to become wealthy—big time adult wealthy. Some of these people look at the standards to join the financial elite and see a starting point. That is, they see US$20 million as a good beginning. As we addressed in *Chapter 3: Money Rules*, there's a proven methodology that can be employed to join the financial elite and even join the ranks of the super-rich and it hinges on the Personal Wealth Creation Program.

Over the last few years, we've been called in to consult and apply this methodology with respect to extreme wealth creation. And, there's every indication that the number of these types of consulting engagements are just starting to rev up.

We've seen a wide variety of situations and the clients tend to fall into three categories. Turnarounds are people who have made and then lost fortunes and strongly desire to be very wealthy again. Lift-offs are the low end of the financial elite who want to be very rich. Extensions are the super-rich who want to create even greater personal fortunes.

From the perspective of the multi-family office, the business opportunities are usually with the formally super-rich and the wealthy who want to expeditiously reach super-rich status. Let's take a look at good candidates for these kinds of consultations and the expertise required to make it all work.

# IDENTIFYING THE GOOD CANDIDATES

There are a number of ways turnarounds and lift-offs are being implemented. Herein, we'll discuss one perspective that has proven to be very efficacious. First, let's understand who's a turnaround or lift-off candidate. A good turnaround or lift-off candidate has the following basic fact pattern:

- A tremendously strong desire to become extremely wealthy again or now.

- The mindset, talents and skills that can be refined and directed on what it's going to take to build or rebuild a fantastic personal fortune.

- A high-quality professional and/or personal network that can be readily and adroitly enhanced and monetized.

- Financial or other resources (e.g., brand, intellectual capital, existing businesses, etc.) that can be innovatively leveraged.

We're seeing a growing number of cases of the once financial elite who are very motivated to reclaim their former economic stature. Some examples include:

- A musician/entrepreneur who let the high-living celebrity lifestyle distract him to the tune of a US$50 million loss while racking up debts twice as high.

- A hedge fund manager caught flat-footed in the credit crisis followed by a disintegrating professional and personal life resulting in having to re-start from ground zero.

- An artist that rode the boom but is now "all over the place" and about to declare personal bankruptcy.

Compared to turnarounds, the number of very successful people who approach us to assist them in creating extreme wealth is considerably greater. A few examples include:

- The managing director of a boutique investment bank seeing that he only has about a decade left to hit it really, really big.

- A highly talented music producer who's watching his less talented "friends" buy jets and palatial mansions all the while badly wanting to join the crowd.

- A highly successful business owner desiring to cultivate a "great fortune" so he can underwrite research looking for a cure for a rare cancer that killed his son.

# REQUISITE EXPERTISE

The basis for all turnarounds and lift-offs are the Money Rules. The development and implementation of a Personal Wealth Creation Program is the foundation for all subsequent action. More to the point, it's the underpinning of nearly every effective attainment of extreme wealth. As discussed, the Money Rules identify the very well trodden path to creating a significant personal fortune.

In each client-specific situation, we work to translate the Money Rules into tactics and specific actions with precise, mutually agreed upon, measurable outcomes. Again, there's a range of application for these "rules of conduct" so a turnaround or lift-off candidate can readily settle for a net worth in the high tens or hundreds of millions as opposed to striving to stand on the apex of the financial pyramid.

Moving beyond the Personal Wealth Creation Program, we find that four types of expertise are often employed when it comes to turnarounds and lift-offs. These types of expertise are housed in many multi-family offices or accessible by them. They are:

- Administrative services.

- Business consulting.

- Advanced planning strategies.

- Private investment banking.

# ADMINISTRATIVE SERVICES

The client often needs to be organized so everyone will know—especially the client—what we're dealing with. This information is required initially and ongoing. Consequently, comprehensive net worth and income statements are required. A cash flow analysis is also in order. All contracts, agreements and understandings need to be reviewed and evaluated. These and related administrative services are therefore core to turnarounds and lift-offs.

# BUSINESS CONSULTING

Generally, we bring directly—or in concert with others—business consulting expertise to the engagement. This regularly involves constructing or evaluating business plans. However, it's more than just an assessment of a business model or a judgment about predicted growth. What's required is to evaluate the business plans from the perspective of private wealth creation. Also, this is where we need to capitalize on the client's personal and professional relationships we previously mapped out.

## ADVANCED PLANNING STRATEGIES

The application of advanced planning strategies is usually essential to maximize the client's personal fortune. By intimately understanding the tax code, we can assist clients to take the vital steps to enhance and protect their wealth as well as be tax-efficient when it comes to the opportunities that will potentially translate into extreme wealth.

## PRIVATE INVESTMENT BANKING

The way many of the business endeavors and other projects will be monetized is transactional. Selling equity positions, for instance, is the primary way to create extreme wealth. Private investment banking has a more expansive definition than simply the buying or selling of equity positions. It can also encompass arranging for financing.

# THE COMPENSATION CONUNDRUM

Turnarounds and lift-offs are always thorny, time consuming and nuanced engage-ments. They can have enormous upside, but they're also often quite expensive to run. As such, there will not be that many firms able or willing to get involved in turnarounds or lift-offs—fewer yet who will be able to be profitable doing so.

The way a multi-family office gets compensated in these situations is a critical determining factor in the viability of the model. What's clear is that an assets under management form of compensation is not tenable. That said, there are a variety of ways the MFO can be compensated such as:

- Retainer fees.

- Transaction fees.

- Project fees.

- Consulting fees.

- Success fees.

- A piece of the action.

The way we structure our turnaround or lift-off engagements is completely dependent on the client's idiosyncratic situation coupled with our assessment of resource commitments and where he or she is likely to end up along a time continuum. More often than not, we adopt a multi-layered offset approach to compensation based on pre-determined metrics. We often need to readjust the compensation arrangement based on how the relationships and the business scenarios evolve.

# THE OPPORTUNITY FOR MULTI-FAMILY OFFICES

A holistic multi-family office is well positioned to deliver the technical expertise required in turnarounds. It's pretty evident that turnarounds and lift-offs, while going to increase as a niche business for MFOs and other boutique advisory firms, will remain a niche business. As with successful corporate turnarounds, successful former financial elite turnarounds are exciting and intellectually stimulating engagements that have enormous profit potential for all involved. The same can be said for lift-offs.

# Specialty Family Offices

I t's no secret that the rich are different and, as a result, require a different type of financial services structure to flourish. We've found, however, that certain types of wealth spawn unique issues that need to be managed carefully; in essence, creating a sub-segment of rich that are even more different than the rest of the wealthy population. In these types of situations, a truly tailored and customized platform of products and services is needed to address their needs—enter the specialty family office. The best example of this, though there are many possible applications within the multi-family office construct, is the Celebrity Family Office.

Backed by talent and focus (and usually a little well-timed luck), some entertainers and professional athletes achieve the kind of success that yields the twin benefits of fame and fortune. Like other wealthy individuals, celebrities have financial needs that can be addressed by the wealth management and support services described herein but they are further distinguished by those issues that are specific to the entertainment and sports businesses, such as royalties or image licensing, that depend on special expertise to achieve financially optimal results.

Celebrities can especially benefit from the coordinated approach characteristic of a multi-family office, one byproduct of which is a staff that is well-versed in the concerns and priorities of a high-profile clientele and can oversee the integration of advanced planning, business strategy and related support services.

## ISSUES FACED BY CELEBRITIES

First, though, let's consider the distinct concerns of celebrities. While most high-profile successes appear to have a charmed life, there is usually an intense back story filled with frustrations and anxieties that cannot be overlooked. Even when they have made it, achieving levels of success long sought in our culture, most find that celebrity status has its drawbacks. For nine out of ten wealthy famous people, the entertainment business is rife with stress (Exhibit 15.1). Three of five are plagued by an intense fear of failure. This can lead to psychological problems—

from drug and alcohol abuse to anxiety and depression (Exhibit 15.2). Complications like these can make their lives more complex and problematic.

**EXHIBIT 15.1:**

## Stress and Failure Among Entertainers

N = 1,045 Entertainers (based on 203 entertainment attorneys)

Source: *Fame & Fortune: Maximizing Celebrity Wealth* (2008)

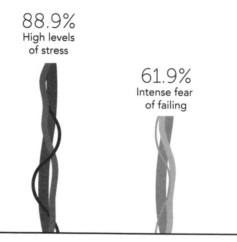

**88.9%**
High levels
of stress

**61.9%**
Intense fear
of failing

**EXHIBIT 15.2:**

## Consequences for Entertainers

N = 1,045 Entertainers (based on 203 entertainment attorneys)

Source: *Fame & Fortune: Maximizing Celebrity Wealth* (2008)

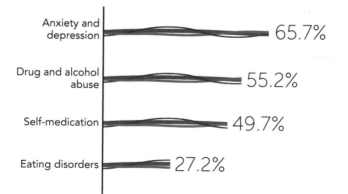

Anxiety and depression — 65.7%

Drug and alcohol abuse — 55.2%

Self-medication — 49.7%

Eating disorders — 27.2%

Athletes don't fare much better. Every move an athlete makes is observed, analyzed, and, frequently, second-guessed by coaches, managers, teammates, members of the press and fans. For many of these professionals, there is a strong relationship between their self-esteem and their ability to perform. When they are not playing at their potential or are struggling with a specific issue, it can undermine their sense of self-worth and tarnish their public image. Since a great number of people and organizations, such as sports federations and commercial sponsors rely on winning athletes to generate revenue it's understandable that most athletes feel the pressure and have an overwhelming fear of failure (Exhibit 15.3). This translates into emotional issues as well as problems with drugs and alcohol (Exhibit 15.4).

EXHIBIT 15.3:

## Intense Fear of Failing

N = 178 Athletes (based on 89 agents)

70.8%
Intense fear
of failure

EXHIBIT 15.4:

## Consequences for Athletes

N = 178 Athletes (based on 89 agents)

46.1%
Emotional
problems

34.8%
Drug and
alcohol abuse

# THE EVOLVING MULTI-FAMILY OFFICE

Because of the great amount of personal wealth that's been created in the last couple of decades, the multi-family office model is evolving in a number of different and intersecting directions. Such offices must increasingly be able to handle a variety of interconnected financial situations. They also have to specialize more if they want to serve specific niche groups, celebrities being just one.

We find that celebrities seeking a financial advisory relationship are increasingly attracted to the multi-family office model, which integrates core aspects of a business manager's job with a broad array of financial and legal expertise. Successful entertainers and athletes are turning to such a business model because the multi-family office can help them navigate their financial worlds and be nimble enough to offer business strategy and support services particular to the entertainment field. To better understand the differences between a traditional multi-family office and a specialty multi-family office, let's look at a couple of examples of advanced planning with celebrities, as well as an example of how the advisors provide business strategy and support.

# ADVANCED PLANNING WITH ENTERTAINERS

Advanced planning is a suite of cutting edge services that help wealthy individuals and families structure their assets to be as tax-effective and secure as possible. The three components of advanced planning—wealth enhancement, estate planning and asset protection—can be offered separately or in concert to deliver the right solution for a successful entertainer (see *Chapter 10: Advanced Planning Services*).

For example, successful entertainers very much want to reduce the amount of money they pay in taxes. Yet only 20% of them have taken steps to curtail these taxes by taking advantage of their unique sources of income.

# Case Study #1

Consider advanced planning leveraging a loan-out corporation. One actor we worked with had a net worth in excess of US$50 million and an annual income of about US$5 million, much of which came from his royalties and participation arrangements. He wanted to lower his income tax bill, so several years ago we established a loan-out corporation for him that was domiciled outside the United States in a country known for its favorable tax treaties. We developed a deferred compensation program within the corporation and directed his non-U.S. royalties and participations into that program. The assets in the deferred compensation program were invested in cash and cash equivalents to safeguard the principal. After one year and one day, this loan-out corporation could make interest- and principal-deferred loans. Loans are made to the actor using the assets in the deferred compensation program as funding; no current taxes are owed on the loans. This solution allows the actor to access his current earnings while decreasing his current tax obligations.

# Case Study #2

Successful entertainers also tend to have certain types of assets particular to the entertainment business that require advanced planning help. Recently, a composer we worked with divorced her husband of 21 years and she owed him a significant lump sum settlement. Her goal was to retain ownership of her song catalog, her largest and most valuable asset, while at the same time meeting the terms of the divorce judgment. We designed a derivative transaction to "convert" the catalog into a security. We hedged the security to create liquidity and invested 80% of the security's total value (in this case, US$24 million) in a guaranteed return investment. A portion of the loan was used to satisfy the composer's obligation in her divorce settlement and pay off the loan. She will retain any residual profits. In five years, we will unwind the structure, at which time the ex-husband will have been paid in full. The composer will have realized US$2.2 million in profit, and she will have complete ownership of her catalog.

# BUSINESS STRATEGY AND SUPPORT

Advisors in specialty multi-family offices can also offer business strategy and support, handling licensing agreements or business ventures with the celebrities' names attached and helping them capitalize on their success to generate significant monies. All too often, advisors will let celebrities not well versed in these areas dive into business deals with a very limited chance of success.

When celebrities call on advisors to develop a business model, it means the advisors must go beyond the role of a traditional multi-family office, beyond the role of a business manager or even that of a management consultant, because they're tackling the client's financial and tax issues all along the way. The client's lifestyle also comes into play.

Let's consider a musician we worked with who wanted to build a company that will profit from purchasing song catalogs. The expertise we brought to the table allowed us to:

- Develop the business plan with the musician, including the pro formas, and adjust the business plan as circumstances changed.

- Arrange preferential financing on an ad hoc and ongoing basis for acquiring music catalogs.

- Assist in the catalog acquisition process to create greater value for both parties while avoiding direct monetary outlays.

- Structure the business to dampen both corporate and personal income taxes by creating a series of tax-friendly current and deferred revenue streams.

- Integrate the business from inception with the celebrity's estate plan to freeze the value of the business's assets and maximize his ability to transfer the value to future generations.

- Protect the ownership rights in the music catalogs from potential litigators and creditors, including ex-spouses.

In this capacity, the celebrity multi-family office is taking on a number of functions simultaneously and seamlessly. What makes it all work so well is the highly integrated nature of the endeavor. In these situations, the objective is not only to have a successful business but to ensure that the wealth of the musician is maximized and protected.

Along the same lines, we're seeing more celebrities who have derailed or celebrities close to "busting out." The former are turnaround situations and the later are lift-off situations (see *Chapter 14: Turnarounds & Lift-offs*). The ability of these celebrities to really create a substantial fortune requires more expertise than what the typical advisory professional or MFO can provide.

# THE ADVANTAGE OF BEING HOLISTIC

Can successful entertainers and athletes work with advanced planning specialists to mitigate taxes? Can celebrities work with business consultants to develop new initiatives? Can successful entertainers and athletes obtain all the expertise of a celebrity multi-family office on an a la carte basis? The answer to all of these questions is: Of course they can.

There are two critical advantages the celebrity multi-family office will have for successful entertainers and athletes. One is an in-depth understanding of the celebrity world. More important, however, is the ability of the multi-family office to address the needs and wants of the successful entertainer and athlete in a holistic manner.

While a top-notch multi-family office will provide solutions to specific issues, problems and needs, it should also be all-encompassing and comprehensive. This will allow it to provide more effective and efficient solutions for the celebrity client whose personal and professional lives are often highly intertwined.

# Leadership Transitions

*Adapted from **Changing of the Guard** by Russ Alan Prince &
Hannah Shaw Grove, sponsored by Rothstein Kass, 2008. Copies of the
complete report are available at www.rkco.com.*

The business of private wealth management is at a critical juncture in its evolution. More multi-family offices are being created and commercial entities, such as brokerages, private banks and independent advisory firms, are forming family office units to compete for the lucrative business of wealthy families by delivering a broad array of capabilities with personalized attention.

As the choices for family office style services has proliferated, many families have chosen to join forces with another family or merge their operations into a multi-family office to pool resources and streamline costs. The expense and oversight required to successfully maintain a single-family office have rendered it a structure that appeals only to the wealthiest and most dedicated of families. When the management and control of an office passes to a younger generation, it's not uncommon to reassess many of the organization's foundation elements against a new suite of criteria, a process that can lead to difficult and transformational decisions. Single-family offices that continue operations in their original construct are experiencing a dramatic shift under the domineering hand of their new leaders.

## THE RESEARCH

Over the course of four years we spoke with single-family offices that had passed from one generation to another in an effort to understand the implications of a leadership change on the organization. In that time we conducted in-depth interviews with nearly 100 global family offices that are now controlled by the second generation of wealth (Exhibit 16.1). The single-family offices in our study had average total assets of nearly US$900 million and median assets of US$685 million (Exhibit 16.2). They were roughly split evenly between being US based and non-US based (Exhibit 16.3).

**EXHIBIT 16.1:**

# Single-Family Offices that Transitioned

N = 94 Single-Family Offices

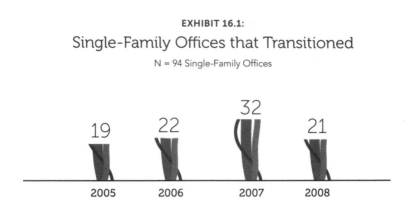

| 19 | 22 | 32 | 21 |
|----|----|----|----|
| 2005 | 2006 | 2007 | 2008 |

**EXHIBIT 16.2:**

# AUM at the Time of Transition (in US$ millions)

N = 94 Single-Family Offices

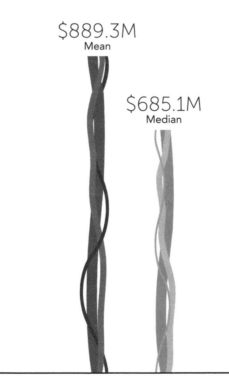

$889.3M
Mean

$685.1M
Median

**EXHIBIT 16.3:**

## Geography

N = 94 Single-Family Offices

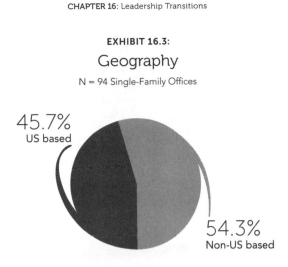

45.7%
US based

54.3%
Non-US based

Our preliminary questions indicated that younger generations had plans to initiate pervasive changes in the office after their ownership transition was complete. The following activities all transpired within six months from the advent of the new management.

## INTENSIFYING THE INVESTMENT FOCUS

Investment management has long been the central focus of most family office structures, and new leadership has reinforced this by increasing the resources dedicated to managing the pooled family assets (Exhibit 16.4). Oversight of the investment process has become even more important as performance returns have disappointed, on both an absolute and relative basis, and ubiquitous high-net-worth products such as hedge funds have struggled with their mandates and attracted more attention from regulators.

**EXHIBIT 16.4:**

## Providing Investment Services

N = 94 Single-Family Offices

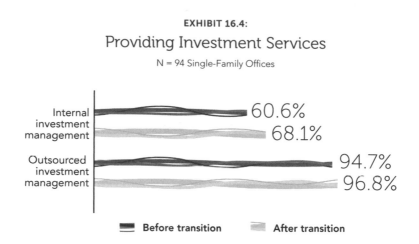

| Internal investment management | 60.6%<br>68.1% |
| Outsourced investment management | 94.7%<br>96.8% |

■ **Before transition**   ■ **After transition**

When push comes to shove, services that are perceived as secondary or tertiary to the primary goal of investment management are sacrificed. The principal administrative and advanced planning services provided by single-family offices were slashed by the organizations in our survey as they struggled with the sometimes competing goals of managing expenses, meeting investment goals and aligning resources (Exhibit 16.5).

**EXHIBIT 16.5:**

## Providing Administrative Services

N = 94 Single-Family Offices

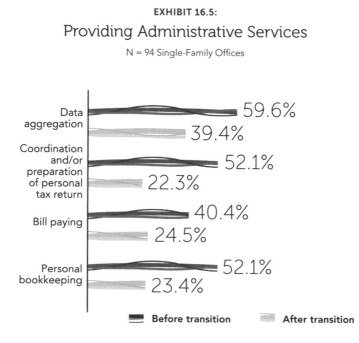

| Data aggregation | 59.6%<br>39.4% |
| Coordination and/or preparation of personal tax return | 52.1%<br>22.3% |
| Bill paying | 40.4%<br>24.5% |
| Personal bookkeeping | 52.1%<br>23.4% |

■ **Before transition**   ■ **After transition**

It's important to note that administrative services and advanced planning are still a critical part of an ultra-wealthy family's overall financial needs, but more family offices are realizing that they can no longer be provided in-house in a cost-effective manner. In most cases, single-family offices are turning to third-party experts to provide specific services on an as-needed basis (Exhibit 16.6).

EXHIBIT 16.6:

## Providing Advanced Planning Services

N = 94 Single-Family Offices

Lifestyle needs, which tend to be more personal in nature, were also moved outside the centralized structure of the single-family office. This decision allows family members to pursue only those that are of interest to them at their own expense, further streamlining the operations and expenses of the organization (Exhibit 16.7).

Two lifestyle services have, however, grown in relevance during the same time— security and healthcare. The interest in security is consistent with trends seen among other segments of the affluent population, and engaging a security consultant to help a family assess its risks, put crisis response plans in place, and design an overall security program is now part of roughly half of single-family offices. This area also shows signs of continued expansion as wealthy individuals fear for the safety of their financial and personal assets.

Likewise, emergency healthcare is often coordinated as part of a broader security initiative and has grown commensurately. This is especially important among families with business interests and real estate in more than one country requiring family members to travel regularly and risk exposure to unexpected physical dangers in locations without immediate access to high quality medical care.

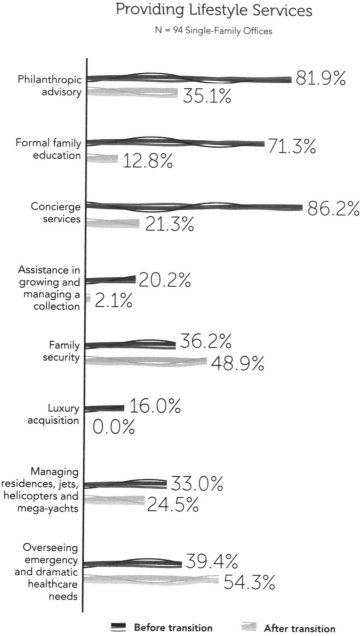

EXHIBIT 16.7:

# Providing Lifestyle Services

N = 94 Single-Family Offices

Philanthropic advisory — 81.9% / 35.1%

Formal family education — 71.3% / 12.8%

Concierge services — 86.2% / 21.3%

Assistance in growing and managing a collection — 20.2% / 2.1%

Family security — 36.2% / 48.9%

Luxury acquisition — 16.0% / 0.0%

Managing residences, jets, helicopters and mega-yachts — 33.0% / 24.5%

Overseeing emergency and dramatic healthcare needs — 39.4% / 54.3%

■ Before transition    ■ After transition

# OUT WITH THE OLD...

Streamlining the operational focus of a single-family office can rarely be achieved without making changes to the professionals, both internal and external, who oversee the related functions (Exhibit 16.8). As such, the younger generations who are now at the helms of their single-family offices are instituting personnel changes they believe will better reflect their priorities and enable them to reach their goals.

This shift in thinking is clearly exemplified in the recruitment of new senior managers to fill the crucial roles that ensure a family office's day-to-day activities match its long-term agenda. In 86% of cases the office's executive director was replaced shortly after a management transition, and 94% of single-family offices brought in a new investment professional to orchestrate all its interrelated financial activities.

**EXHIBIT 16.8:**

## Changes in Key Personnel After Transition

N = 94 Single-Family Offices

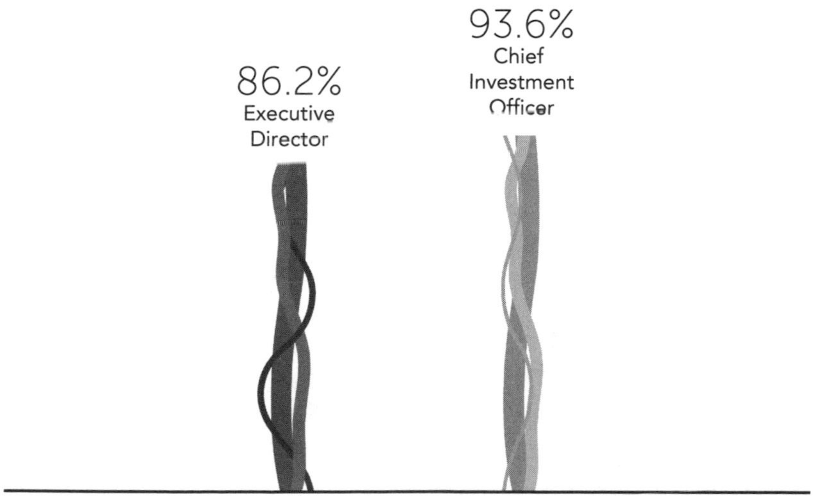

93.6%
Chief
Investment
Officer

86.2%
Executive
Director

Not surprisingly, the offices in our study had an equally high level of turnover among the array of vendors servicing their assets. Approximately nine in ten of the single-family offices released the investment, accounting, legal and banking professionals of their parents and grandparents to seek new counterparts of their own choosing (Exhibits 16.9, 16.10 & 16.11). The reasons behind this all-encompassing change include a desire to:

- Access state-of-the-art strategies and techniques.

- Exert greater control over third-party servicing efforts.

- Cultivate loyalty with a new generation of providers.

- Avoid difficulties stemming from historical relationships and ideals.

- Benefit from more aggressive and competitive pricing.

- Work with younger professionals that relate more successfully to the new generation in charge.

- Help new team members begin working together on equal footing.

**EXHIBIT 16.9:**

## Changes in Key Vendors After the Transition

N = 94 Single-Family Offices

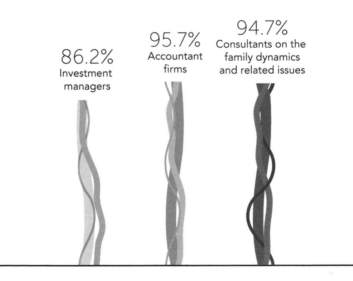

86.2%
Investment
managers

95.7%
Accountant
firms

94.7%
Consultants on the
family dynamics
and related issues

**EXHIBIT 16.10:**

# Changes in Attorneys Used After the Transition

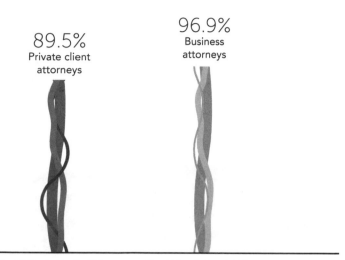

89.5%
Private client
attorneys

96.9%
Business
attorneys

N = 51 Single-Family Offices    N = 62 Single-Family Offices

**EXHIBIT 16.11:**

# Changes in Banking Relationships After the Transition

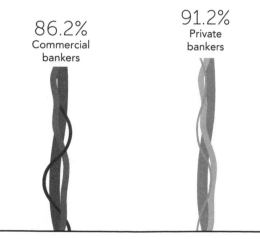

86.2%
Commercial
bankers

91.2%
Private
bankers

N = 94 Single-Family Offices    N = 34 Single-Family Offices

There were far fewer changes in back-office support among the family offices in our study due in part to the commodity-like nature of these services and the terms of existing contracts (Exhibit 16.12).

**EXHIBIT 16.12:**

## Changes in Back-office Support
## After the Transition

43.4%
Trust companies

20.4%
Broker/dealers

9.9%
Technology vendors

N = 58 Single-Family Offices    N = 53 Single-Family Offices    N = 91 Single-Family Offices

## ... IN WITH THE NEW

The generation that established the 94 single-family offices in our survey were heavily influenced by the dynamics of World War II, global expansion and emigration. As a result, many of the offices were built around unique personal perspectives that remained unchanged for the duration of the patriarch's or matriarch's life. Younger generations have typically benefited from higher levels of education and financial success than their forebears, and many of the changes discussed herein are an attempt to infuse that knowledge and experience into an operation that they believe will benefit from a more sophisticated approach (Exhibit 16.13).

# Motivations for the Changes

N = 94 Single-Family Offices

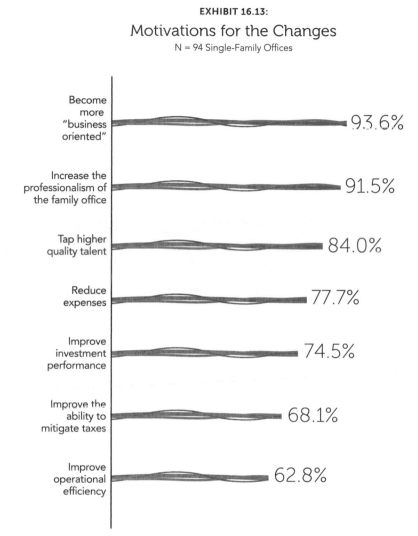

# The Outpost Family Office

Being unable to address every matter, unable to deliver every service at the highest levels of expertise, and being sensitive to the expense side of the equation has led to a strong movement away from building infrastructure and toward outsourcing. We see this in many ways including:

- The use of outside money managers
  (see *Chapter 9: Investment Management*).

- The heavy reliance on outside counsel
  (see *Chapter 10: Advanced Planning*).

- The tighter focus of single-family offices
  when the newer generation takes over
  (see *Chapter 16: Changing of the Guard*).

The ability for family offices—both single- and multi-family offices—to work with outside providers is proving to be increasingly valuable. By creating these relationships, the family offices are able to establish more meaningful relationships with family members or wealthy clients. More importantly, they're able to do a seriously better job in meeting the needs and wants of these high-net-worth people.

Experientially and observationally, we're seeing a new variation on this theme. It has a lot to do with managing costs as well as adding specific expertise. The trend is burgeoning because it's a cost-effective way to provide the highest quality responsiveness and oversight across the world as well as providing on-the-ground supervision of certain types of investments and related activities as well as being able to deliver specific specialized capabilities. We're calling this trend the outpost family office. This is where a single- or multi-family office in one geographic region creates a relationship with a multi-family office in another geographic region.

# THE NEED FOR OUTPOSTS

Grace is a perpetual tourist. As she bounces around the world she needs to address a plethora of cultural, financial and legal issues in a variety of jurisdictions. A multi-family office centered in Europe manages certain critical aspects of her life. The multi-family office has a specialty that is "perpetual tourists." But, to be able to truly deliver the state-of-the-art services and products as well as ensure the highest quality attentiveness would require an enormous organization. Such an entity because of its size and organizational complexity would prove economically self-defeating. That being said, then, "What's the answer?" The answer is the outpost family office model.

This multi-family office has established very intricate and extensive relationships with other multi-family offices throughout the world. These other multi-family offices are the "outposts." The outpost family offices are always on call to work with the clients of the European multi-family office—such as the perpetual tourists—when these individuals are in their corner of the world.

This function of the outpost family office extends to family members of the foreign-domiciled family office living in their jurisdiction. Say the family office is located in the Far East. The grandchildren, for instance, are going to college in the United States. In this situation, the outpost family office provides an array of support services to those grandchildren.

Aside from being on call for the wealthy clients or family members of a family office, an expanding role of the outpost family office is the acquisition and oversight of specific types of investments—principally involving real estate and middle-market companies. In these situations, local (which can be countrywide) coverage and expertise is required. For example, if the client of a multi-family office in Europe wants to buy a company in the United States, with the existence and likely growth of the requisite expertise (see *Chapter 11: Private Investment Banking*), the European multi-family office will probably work through a United States equivalent as opposed to just turning to a traditional investment bank. This is due to the more holistic and comprehensive approach generally taken by multi-family offices.

There are instances when a foreign-domiciled multi-family office creates a relationship with another multi-family office to acquire intellectual property and/or provide expertise that they otherwise would be unable to deliver. What we see is that the outpost family office is delivering a different sleeve of services and products (e.g., advanced planning; Personal Wealth Creation Programs) to the family member or client.

While a new business model for family offices, the outpost family office has considerable potential. Simultaneously, there are many opportunities for these arrangements to go bad. Let's consider how to make the arrangement effective.

# GUIDELINES FOR A SUCCESSFUL
# OUTPOST FAMILY OFFICE

Catering to the financial elite is a people business. No app or new technology is going to replace the need to establish and build rapport with the very wealthy. This same personal connection is central to the arrangement between a foreign-domiciled family office and an outpost.

The newness of this business approach and the demand for confidentiality negates our ability to empirically evaluate the success factors underlying an outpost family office arrangement. Nevertheless, based on our experience in this environment in conjunction with our work structuring and facilitating similar types of joint arrangements between various financial and professional firms, we offer the following guidelines:

- Guideline #1: Ensure a matching philosophical approach to serving the financial elite.

- Guideline #2: Guarantee appropriate knowledge transfer.

- Guideline #3: Specify the level of effort and scope of work.

- Guideline #4: Adopt a reasonable compensation model between the family offices.

## GUIDELINE #1:

### Ensure a matching philosophical approach to serving the financial elite.

The two family offices have to be in-synch. This means the way they work with the financial elite coupled with the way they conceptualize and deliver services and products have to complement each other. Clearly, the foreign-domiciled family office and the outpost family office should have the same orientation—Wealth Creator versus Wealth Preserver. However, the matching philosophical approach should go deeper then that.

Whether it's advanced planning, investment management, private investment banking, administrative services or lifestyle services, the two family offices have to be very much on the same page. But, it's also the service model of the family office. The same level of responsiveness is a necessity.

## GUIDELINE #2:

### Guarantee appropriate knowledge transfer.

The industry success of *Inside the Family Office* was because it was the first book detailing the family office universe. Overall, there's a dearth of viable and meaningful information on this corner of the private wealth universe. Even today, while the spotlight has been shown into this corner, there's very little high-quality information—especially operational information. The best way to learn what works best is still from other family offices. Consequently, among family offices there's a very strong appeal for knowledge transfer. This is proving to be a critical determinant among foreign family offices in selecting a multi-family office or some other type of firm to be an outpost.

This ability to share expertise has proven to go a long way to validating selection decisions. It's value added, resulting in the improvement of family member or client servicing. At the same time, it regularly results in greater business opportunities for both family offices.

## GUIDELINE #3:

### Specify the level of effort and scope of work.

What's essential is that the family office and the outpost have very precisely defined the extent of their relationship. It tends to not be an issue of what can be done, but what should not be done. This often comes up with respect to decisions revolving around clients.

What can be very helpful in this regard is the development of an operational grid. Herein the roles and responsibilities are detailed. Underlying the grid, and noted, are the systems and processes—often depicted graphically—that explain the workflow and key contact personnel.

## GUIDELINE #4:

### Adopt a reasonable compensation model between the family offices.

Central to the effective working arrangement between the foreign-domiciled family office and outpost family office is the compensation model which must be deemed reasonable. We know that it will likely be tweaked along the way if not completely redone as the roles and responsibilities change due to an improved working relationship.

Having constructed a plethora of compensation models in many environments including models between foreign-domiciled family offices and prospective outposts, we recommend following the subsequent four steps:

- **Step #1**: Develop demand estimates.

- **Step #2**: Determine resource requirements.

- **Step #3**: Decide upon requisite strategic and financial returns.

- **Step #4**: Build the payout structure.

The construction of the payout structure is the most "artistic" component of the compensation model. The other steps are very scientific in that they employ agreed upon methodologies. While we'll construct financial analyses and projections, while we know the industry norms and variances, while we'll sometimes even use certain versions of discriminate analysis, in the end, our experience with these scenarios is more powerful.

We're not only dealing with gross numbers. What's even more central is the way money moves between the family offices. We're considering the entire spectrum of possibilities from project and retainer fees to product sales and participations. Hence, determining the payout structure is a negotiation.

What matters is that both parties must be comfortable with the way each financially and strategically benefits. Simultaneously, it's essential to always be aware that the compensation model must be flexible in order to adapt to the certainty of changing circumstances.

# The Mistress of the Universe

# The Mistress of the Universe

By Russ Alan Prince and Hannah Shaw Grove

*Russ would practice for hours every day—day after day after day. He was able to, without any physical exertion, strike a brick and literally shatter it. He could take a 5' tall 4"-by-4" hardwood pole, and hit it so the area around where he struck would explode into a mass of splinters. Despite those demonstrations, when he entered the ring, it would only take a few minutes before he was on the ground and in pain. Iron palm can be devastatingly destructive but it only works if you can hit your opponent. If your opponent strikes first, then follows up with a barrage of kicks and punches, it's hard to recover. And, for Russ, that was always the scenario. Nevertheless, he really loved the training and, back then anyway, he healed quickly. That was before he took a sabbatical because it was healthier to move on.*

It was then that a few of us defined and set the parameters for *The Glass Bead Game.* We took the name from Herman Hesse's literary masterpiece; in his book the exact nature of the game is elusive which made it so very appealing to us. We could make it be what we wanted and we did. Our version of the game was an intellectual exercise of nurturing personal power and translating that power into a personal fortune. Our environment was the perfect one to ethnologically study the successful and wealthy. All we did was critically evaluate how the self-made super-rich thought and acted. Pretty quickly, we were able to strip away the hype and drill down to the core mindsets and behaviors that translated into significant wealth. By looking at the matter within a sociological framework it was easy to identify and prove out the requisite "rules of conduct." Very quickly we moved from *The Glass Bead Game* being a loosely defined concept to an experiment to, eventually, a clear-cut roadmap to the pinnacle of the financial pyramid. For one of us, we'll call her the Mistress of the Universe, it was her life's answer.

## *Playing the Game*

The three of us, sit with the patriarch of a terribly successful family business. While he's never been married or been married three times (we never did get that straight), he has more than a dozen sons. We were introduced to him by his #2 concubine and a close friend of the Mistress. He's quite interested in the Mistress and she's more than happy to be coy, embarrassed, honored and generally delighted in his attention—all at the same time, which is no small trick. We're there to learn and after a lot of alcohol, he's happy to share. Over the next few months, as he becomes more enchanted with the Mistress, he shares his own experiences, letting us move quickly past the big ideas to concentrate on specifics.

He lectures us on how to read people. He instructs us on how to identify and exploit the interconnection between parties. He shows us how to triage the demons and angels in a person's soul. He shows us the mechanics of making a great deal. He explains that the wealthy get their share of the prize and that they're amazingly selfish—but in a good way.

In our conversations with the patriarch, we learn that he starts each and every day thinking of how he will grow his fortune. He focuses on the meetings he will be having and how he will take advantage of the weaknesses in others. He's considered a master negotiator because he defines his criteria for success and unless he achieves his goals, he will always walk away.

The Mistress instinctively gravitated to his approach. Negotiations are about victories. Negotiations are not about fairness, they're about unfairness. It's about achieving the interim goals that are crucial to achieving the ultimate goal—that vast personal fortune. She embraces the art of negotiation as a foundation for her personal development, for her personal power, for her personal wealth.

Together we work out an intricate systematic process that lets her clarify her actions in business situations. This takes a variety of forms. For instance, we develop, with great precision, a structure for how she needs to address each and every aspect of a major negotiation, all the way from setting the stage to managing expectations on the back-end.

We also developed a complex set of procedures to identify all the people who could help her achieve both her interim objectives and the ultimate goal. Another facet of the process is a motivational analysis that allows the Mistress to have a powerful (and definitely unfair) edge.

Though the Mistress has no issue with the other parties doing well in negotiations, they rarely do, so it's no surprise that this approach nets more hostility than friendship. But making other people happy is not the objective, getting sensationally rich is.

About six months after we first sat down together, the Mistress is ready to put our lessons and newfound advantages to use. The patriarch was in the midst of some severe problems that were impacting his personal and professional life and, therefore, his judgment. The result was a prickly arrangement—one that was particularly favorable to the Mistress and left the patriarch with a deal worth mere pennies on the dollar. Once the Mistress owned his company she delivered the final insult: naming her friend, the #2 Concubine, as president of the firm.

## *A Rose By Any Other Name...*

Today we refer to *The Glass Bead Game* by another name: Money Rules. While we saw the "rules of conduct" all those years ago, over the decades we've been able to obtain a more expansive, in-depth and holistic under-standing of the self-made super-rich. These insights and perspectives coupled with years of consulting experiences have enabled us to vastly refine the methodology that can be employed to produce extreme wealth.

As consultants providing guidance on how to play *The Glass Bead Game*, we now refer to the methodology as a *Personal Wealth Creation Program*.

Still, as we reflect on the days when Russ was regularly getting thrashed in the ring, and getting back up for another round of physical punishment, we realize that the essence of the methodology hasn't changed all that much. Moreover, when we search through history for creators of vast personal fortunes, Money Rules is nothing new. People have been playing some version of *The Glass Bead Game* for as long as people have been around.

The biggest difference between then and now is not in the nature of the Money Rules. The biggest difference is in the level of precision we can bring as consultants to wealthy clients who are motivated to build on their vast fortunes. With academic rigor and years of experience behind us, we've been able to develop highly effective and efficacious pedagogical strategies, tools and techniques for mastering the Money Rules.

As for the Mistress, she became phenomenally wealthy and was the main reason Russ took that sabbatical from fighting. One of the most enduring lessons she taught us was perhaps best summed up by Oscar Wilde when he said "True friends stab you in the front."

# Appendix A

## THE ADVISORY MIGRATION

*Adapted from **The Multi-Family Office Solution** by Russ Alan Prince &
Hannah Shaw Grove, sponsored by Rothstein Kass, 2009. Copies of the
complete report are available at www.rkco.com.*

Given the prevalence of asset-based revenues in the advisory field, it's understandable that business strategies offering a path to more consistent client relationships and income irrespective of market and investment performance are being given serious consideration. As competition for the attention and assets of the super-rich mounts, the multi-family office construct offers a more viable and client-focused platform for companies in search of a new business proposition.

Over the five-year period between 2004 and 2008, the average and minimum client assets at U.S. investment advisory firms rose and fell in conjunction with the markets while interest in the multi-family office business model increased steadily (Exhibit A.1).

**EXHIBIT A.1:**

## Advisory Firms from 2004-2008

| Survey date | Sample size | Average client assets (in US$ millions) | Minimum client assets (in US$ millions) | % want to become Multi-family offices |
|---|---|---|---|---|
| 2004 | 206 | $22.6 | $6.4 | 48.1% |
| 2005 | 198 | $19.8 | $7.2 | 51.5% |
| 2006 | 216 | $35.4 | $9.1 | 65.3% |
| 2007 | 179 | $31.7 | $12.2 | 68.2% |
| 2008 | 244 | $16.9 | $6.1 | 71.3% |

The top five reasons driving interest in the multi-family office structure are interconnected, with most firms anticipating that a broader platform of capabilities and a higher-touch service model that allows for greater personalization will ultimately lead to stronger client satisfaction, higher profitability, greater competitiveness, and more qualified referral prospects (Exhibit A.2).

**EXHIBIT A.2:**
## Motivations to Become a Multi-Family Office

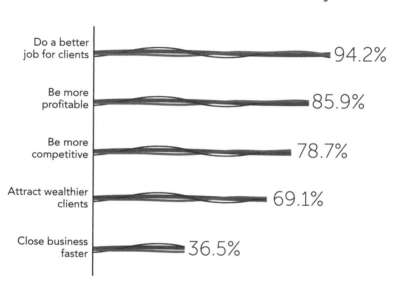

The worsening fiscal conditions of the past several years have helped to highlight the flaws inherent in the structure and operations at many financial institutions. In addition to weathering the harsh scrutiny from regulators, taxpayers and the media, most firms are looking for ways to shore up existing business and expand. The multi-family office has emerged as a suitable evolution for an industry that aspires to a wealthier, and potentially more profitable, clientele and the business premise has been variously interpreted and adopted by a growing faction. From the wealthy client's perspective, it's an effective choice—but it remains unclear whether this dedicated and highly-tailored approach can thrive under conventional management oversight and the auspices of the financial mainstream.

# Appendix B

## SELECTING A MULTI-FAMILY OFFICE

A family office can play a central role in how a family coalesces around its wealth, so finding the right firm is critical. This is especially important given the recent, and growing, adoption of the multi-family office business model by financial services providers in an effort to strenghten their affluent client relationships, be more profitable and separate themselves from the competition.

The financial elite are well versed in the art of the referral and typically turn to someone they trust to provide them with an introduction—whether it's to a massage therapist, a criminal attorney or a yacht broker—as a way of mitigating risk. A referral implies both the personal experience and endorsement of the person making the introduction thereby decreasing the chance of encountering inexperience or incompetence. In the case of financial services, because the offerings are often intangible and complex, a referral can help an individual or family locate the organizations and experts that have a good track record and have an outstanding reputation among their peers.

A referral, however, is only the first step in finding a multi-family office. Once a potential provider has been identified, it is up to the family and their closest advisors and associates to conduct their own assessment and control the selection process. Following these guidelines can help ensure a good fit between a family and a multi-family office.

1. **Integrity:** The strongest relationships are built on a foundation of trust and honesty, so a family office should be both scrupulous and transparent in its actions and motivations.

2. **Expertise**: Successfully managing a sizable portfolio and all the associated issues calls for a team of talented, leading-edge professionals to maximize opportunities and minimize exposures.

3. **Networked:** Even the most adept technicians can't know all the nuances of every strategy, so the best firms have an established network of specialists to call upon for unique situations.

4. **Client-centric:** A high-quality family office will have employees who take the time to really understand a client's goals and concerns, and who are proactive and responsive when they interact with the family members.

5. **In-synch:** Ideally, families will find an organization with which they share a philosophical and practical approach to matters large and small, especially those that can affect the security and well-being of the extended family unit.

6. **Experience:** There's no substitute for the knowledge and insights gathered from hands-on work with the ultra-affluent and their financial affairs; an established and experienced multi-family office will have long-term, satisfied and successful relationships with its high-net-worth clients and industry partners.

7. **Specialization:** Given the desire for personalized service and customized solutions, multi-family offices should be evaluated for their ability to help a family meet its particular goals—including those discussed elsewhere in this book such as wealth preservation or the regeneration of a personal fortune.

## EXECUTIVE DIRECTOR COMPENSATION
## AT SINGLE-FAMILY OFFICES

This section provides details on the 2008 compensation structures for Executive Directors at 376 single-family offices. The average Executive Director earned US$1.8 million and the median compensation was US$850,000 (Exhibit C.1). It's important to note that the majority of the total compensation figure is from bonus, rather than base salary, similar to the pay structures used at investment banks.

**EXHIBIT C.1:**

## Total 2008 Compensation

N = 376 Single-Family Offices

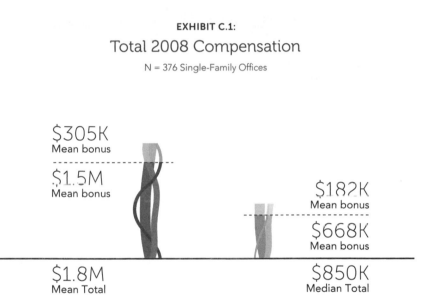

$305K
Mean bonus

$1.5M
Mean bonus

$182K
Mean bonus

$668K
Mean bonus

$1.8M
Mean Total

$850K
Median Total

When the data is segmented by the orientation of the family office, we see that base salaries for Executive Directors are fairly consistent across firms while the 2008 bonuses paid by Wealth Creators were, on average, more than seven times greater than those paid by Wealth Preservers (Exhibit C.2).

**EXHIBIT C.2:**

# Compensation by Orientation

N = 376 Single-Family Offices

## Wealth Creators

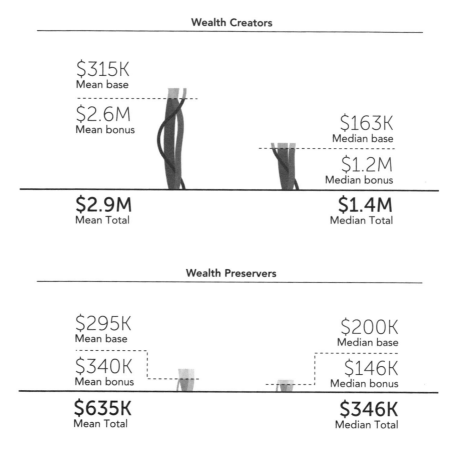

$315K
Mean base

$2.6M
Mean bonus

$163K
Median base

$1.2M
Median bonus

**$2.9M**
Mean Total

**$1.4M**
Median Total

## Wealth Preservers

$295K
Mean base

$200K
Median base

$340K
Mean bonus

$146K
Median bonus

**$635K**
Mean Total

**$346K**
Median Total

# PAYOUT MODELS

Through our research, we've found that there are differences in the way Executive Directors operate and that impacts how they are employed and compensated. Executive Directors of single-family offices are compensated in one of two ways: as an employee of the family performing a task in exchange for a salary or as a participant in the business and/or in specific deals. Roughly two-thirds of Executive Directors are characterized as employees and the balance are defined as participants (Exhibit C.3).

**EXHIBIT C.3:**

## Payout Model

N = 376 Single-Family Offices

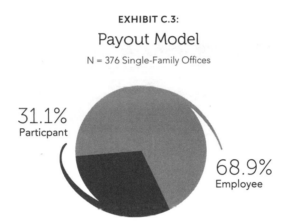

31.1%
Particpant

68.9%
Employee

On average, Participant Directors earned roughly ten times what Employee Directors earned during the same time frame (Exhibit C.4). In fact, the compensation of Employee Directors was fairly constant regardless of the investment orientation of the family office where they were employed (Exhibits C.5 and C.6). Not surprisingly, there is a premium paid to Participant Directors at family offices oriented toward wealth creation, where they earned an average of twelve times more than the Employee Directors at similar firms and roughly twice what the Participant Directors at wealth preservation firms earned.

**EXHIBIT C.4:**

# Compensation by Payout Model

N = 376 Single-Family Offices

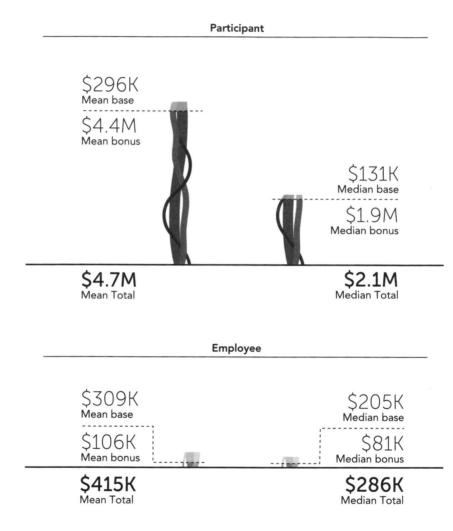

**Participant**

$296K
Mean base

$4.4M
Mean bonus

$131K
Median base

$1.9M
Median bonus

**$4.7M**
Mean Total

**$2.1M**
Median Total

**Employee**

$309K
Mean base

$106K
Mean bonus

$205K
Median base

$81K
Median bonus

**$415K**
Mean Total

**$286K**
Median Total

# Compensation by Wealth Creator and Payout Model

N = 185 Single-Family Offices

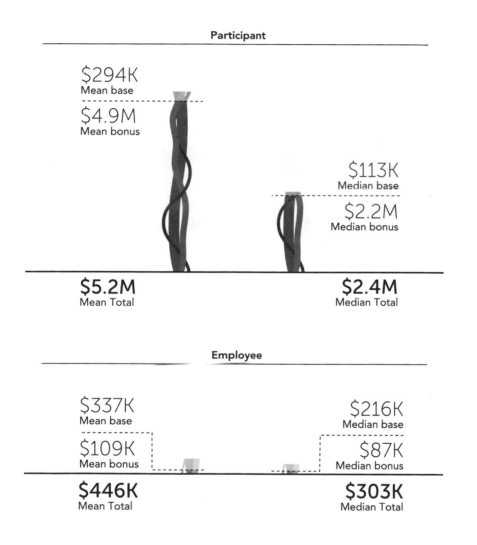

### Participant

$294K
Mean base

$4.9M
Mean bonus

$113K
Median base

$2.2M
Median bonus

$5.2M
Mean Total

$2.4M
Median Total

### Employee

$337K
Mean base

$109K
Mean bonus

$216K
Median base

$87K
Median bonus

$446K
Mean Total

$303K
Median Total

EXHIBIT C.6:

# Compensation by Wealth Preserver and Payout Model

N = 191 Single-Family Offices

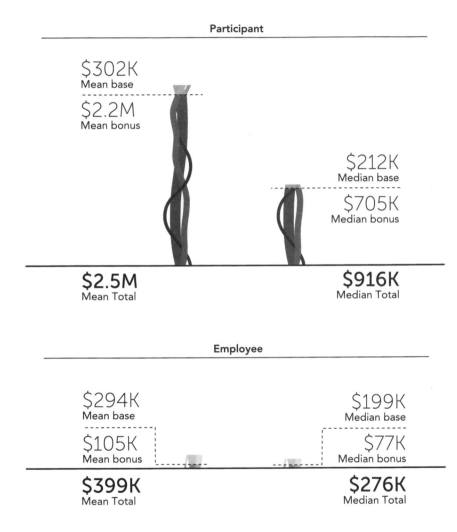

**Participant**

$302K
Mean base

$2.2M
Mean bonus

$212K
Median base

$705K
Median bonus

$2.5M
Mean Total

$916K
Median Total

**Employee**

$294K
Mean base

$199K
Median base

$105K
Mean bonus

$77K
Median bonus

$399K
Mean Total

$276K
Median Total

# Appendix D

## THE WHOLE CLIENT MODEL

The Whole Client Model is an empirically derived profiling mechanism developed from the best practices of the leading financial professionals and other high-end practitioners. When used correctly, this process helps MFOs gain an intimate level of knowledge about their clients, uncover new business opportunities, and act in a more consultative capacity. The model consists of seven interdependent sections that collectively represent a client's complete state of affairs.

EXHIBIT D.1:

### The Whole Client Model

**Client** | Identify the facts that will form the basis of the client's profile, such as age, gender, income, net worth, and other relevant demographics.

**Relationships** | Understand the relationships that are most important to the client and those that carry some financial or emotional obligation.

**Financials** | Understand the client's current sources of income and any factors that may impact him or her in the short-or intermediate-term, as well as the structure, registration and location of assets and liabilities.

**Advisors** | Know all the advisors that work with the client on a regular basis, including accountants, attorneys and business managers, and understand the role and influence each has in his or her life.

**Process** | Understand the client's preferred method and frequency of interaction, and the level of detail required to satisfy his or her sophistication and curiosity.

**Interests** | Identify those activities and topics that occupy the client's time and money, including hobbies, religious, political, medical and philanthropic.

**Goals & Objectives** | Understand the client's personal and professional goals, and his or her intentions for family and loved ones.

# Appendix E

## SAMPLING METHODOLOGY

In studying any select or limited population—any segment of wealth, such as jet owners or family offices, for instance—we do not engage in probability sampling. Instead we employ a non-probability sampling process commonly referred to as snowball sampling. The difference between non-probability and probability sampling is that the former does not involve random selection while the latter does. This does not mean that non-probability samples are not representative of the population; it does mean that non-probability samples cannot depend upon the rationale of probability theory.

With a probabilistic sample, the odds or probability that the population is represented can be computed; the confidence intervals for the statistics can be estimated. With non-probability samples, there is a risk that the population is not estimated well even though statistical controls are applied. When possible, probabilistic or random sampling methods are preferred over non-probabilistic ones. However, it is accepted practice in applied social science research to employ non-probability sampling approaches in circumstances where it is not feasible, practical or theoretically sensible to do random sampling.

Broadly, non-probability sampling methods can be divided into two broad types: accidental or purposive. Snowball sampling, like most sampling methods, is purposive in nature because the sampling problem is approached with a specific plan in mind. In non-probability purposive sampling, sampling is performed with one or more specific predefined groups in mind, such as the Executive Directors in this book.

Purposive sampling is very useful for situations in which a targeted sample cannot be cost-efficiently reached using probability methods. The risk of non-probability purposive sampling is that subgroups in the target population that are more readily accessible may be overweighted. Non-probability purposive sampling approaches include modal instance sampling, expert sampling, quota sampling and heterogeneity sampling as well as snowball sampling.

While snowball sampling was necessary to access the single- and multi-family office universe, it's important to recognize that the research presented in this book was designed and conducted as a business-to-business—one professional entity to another—initiative. While there are a small percentage of wealthy individuals running their own single-family office and can speak as either a member of the high-net-worth population or a representative of the family office, by-and-large, Executive Directors are "employees" of the single- or multi-family offices they represent, as was the case with our study.

# ABOUT THE AUTHORS

 **Russ Alan Prince** is the president of Prince & Associates, Inc., one of the leading high-net-worth research firms, and an authority on private wealth creation and preservation.
www.russalanprince.com

 **Hannah Shaw Grove** is a highly-regarded specialist on the mindset, behaviors and finances of the ultra-affluent and consults to a select group of individuals and professionals.
www.hsgrove.com

 **Keith M. Bloomfield** is the president and chief executive officer of the Forbes Family Trust and a veteran of the wealth management business.
www.forbesfamilytrust.com

 **Richard J. Flynn** is head of the Rothstein Kass Family Office Group and an expert on the sophisticated financial and lifestyle needs of the world's wealthiest families.
www.rkco.com